The Anatomy of Addiction

Overcoming the Triggers that Stand in the Way of Recovery

Morteza Khaleghi, PhD, and
Karen Khaleghi, PhD

palgrave
macmillan

First published in 2011 by
PALGRAVE MACMILLAN®
in the United States—a division of St. Martin's Press LLC,
175 Fifth Avenue, New York, NY 10010.

Where this book is distributed in the UK, Europe and the rest of the world,
this is by Palgrave Macmillan, a division of Macmillan Publishers Limited,
registered in England, company number 785998, of Houndmills,
Basingstoke, Hampshire RG21 6XS.

Palgrave Macmillan is the global academic imprint of the above companies
and has companies and representatives throughout the world.

Palgrave® and Macmillan® are registered trademarks in the United States,
the United Kingdom, Europe and other countries.

ISBN: 978–0–230–10709–0

Library of Congress Cataloging-in-Publication Data

Khaleghi, Morteza.
    The anatomy of addiction : overcoming the triggers that stand in the
way of recovery / Morteza Khaleghi and Karen Khaleghi.
        p. ; cm.
    Includes index:
    ISBN 978–0–230–10709–0
    1. Compulsive behavior—Etiology. 2. Substance abuse—Etiology.
3. Compulsive behavior—Patients—Rehabilitation. 4. Substance abuse—
Patients—Rehabilitation. I. Khaleghi, Karen. II. Title.
    [DNLM: 1. Behavior, Addictive—etiology. 2. Behavior, Addictive—
rehabilitation. WM 176]
RC533.K47 2011
616.86—dc22   2011005458

A catalogue record of the book is available from the British Library.

Design by Newgen Imaging Systems (P) Ltd., Chennai, India.

First edition: October 2011

10 9 8 7 6 5 4 3 2 1

Printed in the United States of America.

Contents

INTRODUCTION

❧

Where the Journey Begins

*I*NTERSTATE 90 IS the longest interstate highway in America. Its 3,100 miles span the continent from Boston, Massachusetts, to Seattle, Washington. Along its westward way, it passes through New York State, following the coastline of Lake Erie to Syracuse, Rochester, and Buffalo. It slices through a short stretch of Pennsylvania—just under fifty miles' worth of the Keystone State—before it swings into Ohio, past Cleveland and the route's most notorious section, a wholly unexpected ninety-degree turn known for good reason as Dead Man's Curve. It ribbons through Indiana, the "Main Street of the Midwest," toward the Chicago Skyway—nearly eight soaring miles and over two billion cumulative dollars of elevated roadway. It rolls through the hills and forests of Wisconsin; crosses into Minnesota farmlands over the great, wide Mississippi; and weaves through South Dakota's prairies before it passes into Wyoming, where the sky really is so big that it can feel as if you're driving in the clouds. In Montana, it crosses the continental divide just east of Butte and jogs north into Idaho where, in the small town of Wallace, it comes to a brief stop at the only traffic light you will encounter on the whole road, coast to coast. In Washington State, it crosses Lake Washington over two of the longest floating bridges in the world, offering a few final knockout views of America's diverse beauty before it reaches its terminus in Seattle.

A trip across the United States on I-90 can be as romantic and surprising an adventure as any traveler wants to make it. But what does a leisurely road trip on America's northernmost interstate have to do with helping people overcome addiction?

Think of I-90 for a moment as a living thing—a life filled with sharp turns, sudden stops, side trips, and long lonely stretches, as well as meandering, breathtaking beauty. What makes I-90 even more ripe for comparison to a life trajectory is that when construction began on the road in 1957, many of its sections were made out of existing byways, so it's a guessing game as to whether the road ahead will have two lanes, or four, or six—or where a tollbooth might pop up, where a speed limit might change abruptly, or where a pothole might be left untended by whatever local authority is in charge of road upkeep along any specific stretch. Like life, it can be a highly uneven passage.

Now think of the events of a life strung out like the cities and towns all along the great interstate. As surely as a baby has to learn to stand on two feet before she can take her first wobbly steps, a westbound traveler starting out on the I-90 lifeline must pass through Toledo before she gets to Fort Wayne; the milestones are as distinct as the landmarks, laid down unalterably in time and space.

But all cities aren't created equal. Some are more attractive and pleasant than others. You may find yourself loath to leave the stunning Snite Museum of Art on Notre Dame's campus in South Bend, but later you are eager to get out of the blinding snowstorm that strands you in a roach motel a few hundred miles up the road. So every phase of life isn't quite equal, either. Every one of us has lived through turmoil that makes a certain week, month, or even year a time in our lives that we would not willingly revisit, just as, indeed, most of us have spent at least one stretch surrounded by such joy and satisfaction that we look back with an aching sense of nostalgia, wishing for all we are worth that we could time travel back there for just a day.

Whether we want to go back or not, however, the cities that we have passed on our journey are still behind us—their concrete and glass and asphalt as sturdy and vivid as the memories we have taken from them. For better or for worse, our trajectory is forever connected to them. And no matter how relieved we are to leave a snowstorm behind and pass out of Indiana and into Chicago, where we have scored tickets to a Bears game or a taping of *Oprah*, when we realize that in our hurry to get away we've left our luggage behind in the lobby of the roach motel, we really have no choice but to go back and collect our things. A cell phone, a favorite outfit, the wallet containing all of our cash and credit cards—there's something we need to retrieve before we can freely and confidently go on our way.

The individual events of our lives are as completely connected to our whole lives as the individual towns and cities are connected to the complete thoroughfare through northern America. What we have lived through makes us what we are. We worked hard to get good grades in school because our parents were hardworking; we admired them and wanted to be like them and make them proud. Or perhaps the reason we worked hard in school was because our parents' lives were bleak; we wanted something better for ourselves and knew that an education was the key to not having to live the same sort of lives they did. This sort of continuum is simply a fact, and in this truth, Dr. K. and I are no different. Certainly Dr. K. was influenced in his choice of psychiatry as his profession by his brother's struggle with undiagnosed clinical depression. When I took my first psychology class as a sophomore in high school, the dysfunction in my family began to make sense to me. I craved a deeper understanding—to learn the effects of multigenerational addiction and how they worked to undermine my own family, and eventually to pass this knowledge on to others who were suffering as I had—so psychology became my life's work. There is a context for everything we do.

In this book, we are going to help you see addiction in a nontraditional light: within the context of the addict's life. Whether the addiction is to drugs, alcohol, sex, gambling, food, shopping, or any other compulsive and destructive behavior, addiction does not become a part of anyone's life struggle out of the blue any more than San Antonio, Texas, or Santa Fe, New Mexico, suddenly appears at an exit ramp on I-90. There is always—*always*—a contextual reason for addiction. Perhaps some traumatic event or some physiological or psychological disease preceded the addiction and, years and even decades later, still causes hurt and distress the sufferer seeks to salve. Drugs or alcohol or sex or gambling, overeating that causes obesity as well as bulimia, obsessive shopping, and even obsessive cigarette smoking—these are all some of the ways that the patient seeks to self-medicate and so mediate her lingering, insistent emotional pain. We are going to help you see how guiding an addict from point to point, dot to dot along his life's trajectory—through sharp turns and sudden stops and side trips, retracing steps and retrieving lost luggage and sorting through it—can give him the power to move forward confidently, free from addiction.

CHAPTER 1

Reframing the Vocabulary of Addiction

BLAME AND SHAME

Lewis came to Creative Care as many of our patients do—at the end of his rope, at the very end of hope. He was in his mid-fifties then, an intelligent and gentle man who, in spite of having already "successfully" completed several other traditional in-patient treatment programs, was unable to string together even a few months of sobriety. What he had managed to string together over the years was a series of arrests for driving under the influence and court appearances, along with mounting legal expenses. He was addicted to both alcohol and prescription medications, and he suffered from a chronic knee problem that he used to explain away his ongoing "need" for pain medications.

Lewis lived on the proceeds of a trust fund his family had set up for him through a family business. While the establishment of the fund could be interpreted as a generous act, in truth it was the result of the family giving up on him; neither his elderly parents nor any of his siblings found much of a reason to believe that Lewis would ever be able to support himself. Within his family, Lewis was a joke, and he'd learned over the years to see himself through their eyes; he couldn't take himself seriously, either. In addition to his other problems, Lewis was morbidly obese, but even in his crippling weight condition, he found fodder for jokes on himself: "Just call me 'the Titanic!'" he told us the first time we met him.

We begin with Lewis's story not because it is sensational but because, in many of its particulars, it is all too common. If you or a loved one has struggled with addiction issues, you'll likely recognize yourself in at least parts of Lewis's story: the exasperation of family, friends, and even coworkers; the periodic brushes with the law; the addict's empty promises and justifications, lack of self-esteem and abundance of health problems, repeated relapses, and the steady escalation of the downward spiral. It doesn't matter if the addiction is to alcohol and prescription medications, as in Lewis's case, or to illegal drugs, gambling, sex, food, shopping, Internet porn, or any other compulsive dependence—the results of addiction are heartbreakingly similar. And the relapse rate of addicts who are treated for their problems in traditional rehabilitation programs remains similarly heartbreakingly high—fully 70 to 90 percent of patients who complete a traditional rehabilitation program are likely to relapse within the first year.[1]

Let us put that dry statistic into some flesh-and-blood perspective. According to the National Institutes of Health (NIH), 17.6 million adults in the United States are alcoholics or suffer from alcohol-related problems.[2] According to a report by the Mayo Clinic, an additional 19.5 million Americans over the age of twelve abuse illegal drugs on a regular basis.[3] Two million individuals are compulsive gamblers.[4] The Society for the Advancement of Sexual Health (SASH) estimates that 3 to 5 percent of the U.S. population could meet the criteria for sexual addiction and compulsivity[5]—that's upward of fifteen million individuals[6]—and SASH considers that the estimate, based on the number of individuals who seek treatment, is a conservative one. Taking into consideration just these four manifestations of addiction, that's thirty-five to forty-five million real, flesh-and-blood people in the United States alone who continue to suffer, year to year, with an addiction problem. Clearly we need a more effective approach to help these people take control of, and overcome, their addictions.

Dr. K. and I have a combined total of over forty-two years implementing this more effective approach. One of the core reasons that our approach works so well is that we move quickly to relieve our patients—and, importantly, our patients' families—of the concept of "blame" or "fault" that too frequently hampers recovery. Lewis's family, for example, had long been invested in the idea that it was Lewis's weakness that caused him to drink and take drugs. They believed that if Lewis was simply more committed to his recovery and had a greater strength of character he could remain sober. But if a patient were brought into an emergency room with a broken leg, no one would blame the patient for his suffering, would they? Similarly, we do not blame—or shame—the addict for the anguish his disease has wreaked. We start by looking at addiction not from the perspective of the *disease* but in the context of the individual addict's *life* and what happened within that life that caused addiction to manifest.

Now, this isn't a revolutionary approach. Most traditional treatment programs revolve around a set of twelve steps on the order of the justly renowned twelve steps of Alcoholics Anonymous (AA). Counselors in these programs help their patients to focus on their subjugation to alcohol, take a fearless inventory of themselves, and seek "through prayer and meditation to improve their conscious contact with God,"[7] as each individual understands him or her. And AA, too, approaches addiction with the sort of compassion that is so necessary to healing ("At my own first meeting in 1982, I felt as shy as Boo Radley, having lived for years in the dark basement of my addiction and shame"[8]), helping the addict emerge from the shadow of disgrace and dishonor his disease has likely cast over him and into the forgiving (and *self-forgiving*) frame of mind in which renewal can happen. This twelve-step structure has proved to be so successful that, indeed, it is an essential part of the treatment we provide at Creative Care; it is also our heartiest recommendation for a long-term sobriety strategy to our discharged patients. It provides the patient with a support system in the form of daily meetings and sponsors that can be key to sustained recovery.

But the twelve steps, as critical and key as they are, are rarely the answer in and of themselves for most addicts. The problem is—and this problem is made stunningly clear in the indisputably dismal relapse rates—that the examination of a client's emotional history prescribed in the twelve steps does not go deep enough. And, all too frequently, it doesn't even touch upon underlying physiological or psychological issues that, left untreated, will sabotage sobriety as surely as night follows day.

But we don't want to get ahead of our story. In order to help you understand the approach that has proven to be so effective at Creative Care, we need to spend a few pages on the vocabulary of addiction, reframing and reforming the language that most of us have used in the past to define addiction and its treatment. There are three phrases to which we want you to pay particular attention because they represent three key concepts to helping our patients—and your loved ones—become free from addiction: *cause and effect, dual diagnosis,* and *locus of control.*

CAUSE AND EFFECT

By the time we make it through the first month or so of first grade, most of us have a pretty keen grasp of what happens if we don't study for our spelling tests. *Chickun. Tabel. Perple.* In short order, we come to understand that to raise our test scores, we must study. We make the connection between preparation and the big red grade mark at the top of our paper.

Causality is the relationship between one event (a cause) and a subsequent event that is a consequence of the first event (an effect). Although we may not consciously think about our everyday lives in quite this way, we spend much of our time learning about and negotiating the delicate, ongoing balance between cause and effect. The effects of our actions can be positive—you bring your wife a bouquet of her favorite flowers for no reason other than you know it will put a smile on her face. Or, we may do what we do simply to avoid a negative situation—no matter how tired you are when you get home from a day at the office, you make time to take the dog out for a walk because none of us likes to deal with the consequences of a cooped-up canine. Either way, in these simple examples, it's easy—intuitive, really—to grasp the connection between our behaviors and the results we can expect from them.

But what happens when the situation we're talking about becomes more complicated? Say that you're a first-grade teacher who has used up just about all of your patience admonishing a bright student who, if only she'd spare a few minutes every evening on her weekly spelling word list, would absolutely get better grades than the 60s and 70s she has been pulling in. As a teacher, you want to reinforce the connection between effort and result, right? But let's say that you are a teacher who is very good at what you do: *You want to know what it is that prevents your bright students from success.* What you find out is that the child is unable to spend those few minutes at home in the evenings concentrating on her word list because her parents are fighting all the time, yelling at each other so she hears them even when she retreats to her own room; her home is not a place that's peaceful and conducive to concentration. What is cause and what is effect suddenly becomes just a little more problematic.

Our conventional thought process is linear. It moves as if there is only one direction in which to go: forward—that is, one thing following upon another. If I do Thing A, then Thing B will happen. As a first-grade teacher, you might begin your attempts to help your underachieving student by thinking in a conventionally linear way about the student's poor spelling-test results—and there's nothing inherently wrong with that. It's clear, linear thinking that gets us through most of our ordinary daily routines—it allows us to, say, recognize that if we don't fill up the gas tank in our car before we head out on a long road trip on I-90 (Thing A), then eventually we'll be stuck sitting on the side of the highway waiting for a tow truck (Thing B).

But a smart teacher will quickly recognize that she began her analysis with the wrong Thing A. It wasn't the lack of good study habits that led to her student's dismal spelling-test grades; it was the lack of a favorable home environment that kept the student from being able to study, which then led to the student's failing marks. That is, the lack of studying wasn't the *cause* of the student's bad grades—it was the *effect* of a traumatic situation in the student's home. Now—here is the crucial part—the teacher could have cajoled, insisted, and warned the student to study until her voice was hoarse, but if the home situation wasn't addressed and altered, the student would likely have fallen further and further behind because she wouldn't ever have had the opportunity to sit peacefully with her homework assignments.

The teacher in our example was able, through training and experience, to alter her thinking pattern and drill deeper into the situation in order to be of real help to her student.

But the conventional thinking about addiction is often haplessly, stubbornly linear—and nearly always starts off at the wrong Thing A.

Societies at large, as well as addicts themselves, their loved ones, and many of the physicians and therapists who treat them, think of addiction as a *cause*. Be*cause* of a person's addiction, he or she can't keep a job, can't sustain relationships, suffers increasing and/or chronic health problems, and brushes up again and again against the wrong side of the law.

Of course, all of these problems may well be part of an addict's life. In fact, it is rare to find someone who is, for example, an alcoholic or a habitual gambler who enjoys long-term employment, a strong marriage, excellent physical health, and a clean police record. But simply putting an addict through his detox paces in a conventional 28-day rehabilitation program is a recipe for relapse. Assuming that an addict, once free of physiological addiction and well schooled about how harmful addiction is in general, should be able to return to the larger world and acquire all of those elements that we traditionally think of as composing "the good life" is setting him up for failure.

The reason that the relapse rate is a shocking 70 to 90 percent for patients who have completed conventional treatment programs is that most conventional treatment programs view the nature of addiction from an old-fashioned perspective—as a physical condition not unlike heart disease or diabetes. As a result, these programs ask the cause-and-effect questions of addiction in a superficial way. At Creative Care, we turn around the conventional thinking and start our inquiry into a patient's recovery by focusing on her addiction as an *effect*. We ask what happened prior to the addiction that caused the patient's need to compulsively—self-destructively—self-medicate. Can the addictive behavior be traced to a life trauma—the death of a parent at a young age, perhaps, or combat duty in the military? Both of these traumas can precede a diagnosis of post-traumatic stress disorder (PTSD). Is the addictive behavior the result of—or exacerbated by—a preexisting psychiatric disorder, such as bipolar disorder, depression, or schizophrenia?

Getting to what happened in a patient's life prior to the manifestation of addiction is not simple or easy work. When patients first come to us, they are nearly uniformly fixated on the here and now of their physical pain and are connected with their emotional pain on merely a surface level.

Let us propose an example that will give you insight into the sort of profound disconnect we are talking about. Let's say that you work for a company that uses annual employee evaluations to determine issues of salary and promotion, and you have just received an unexpectedly negative evaluation from your supervisor. How will you handle the negative emotions generated by the bad review from your boss? Will you dig in and redouble your efforts to do the job right? Or will you huff out of her office and into the nearest bar to soothe your hurt feelings with a glass of wine? And, in either case, will you understand the connection between the emotions you're feeling and the manner in which you are reacting to them?

Although your desire for a glass of cabernet in this instance may not in itself indicate an addiction issue, it can serve as a peek into the addict's dilemma. How many times have you said—or heard someone else say—that you "really need" a drink after a hard day at the office? Making such a statement is making a conscious connection between a stressful situation and your need to take action to immediately relieve the pain of it.

Stress relief does not ideally, of course, come in the form of a glass of wine. The iconic commercial tagline, "Calgon, take me away!" is an almost breathless voice-over to accompany the visual of a harried mom slipping gratefully into a bathtub full of bubbles. A bath is a different form of stress relief, but the commercial makes an unmistakable connection between the events of a difficult day and reprieve.

For an addict, the connection between cause and effect, pain and relief, is rarely, if ever, so clear. When a patient first comes to us, he is unable to make the connection between how he feels and how he behaves. He simply knows that he is in pain and that the pain is intolerable. His life's focus has become to mask the pain through drugs, alcohol, or other addictive behaviors. Our job is to help the patient, and his family, connect the dots between the emotions he is feeling—or, even more accurately, has spent a lifetime avoiding—and the behaviors he is exhibiting.

While this work is neither simple nor easy, it is often exactly the work that the patient himself is crying out to do. When Lewis first came to Creative Care, for instance, he had a lot of *why*s on his mind. Why, even after so many attempts at rehabilitation, had he been unsuccessful at staying sober? Why did he keep hurting himself with alcohol and prescription medication—and food? Why had he been unable to keep the promises he made to his parents, his siblings, and himself? Like many of our patients, Lewis knew intuitively that there were questions that required answers, but he had only a vague notion of what they might be. Like many of our patients, he put the blame for his current family and health and legal problems squarely on his addiction. Our job was to help him see that he was starting with the wrong Thing A and to take him back a bit further on his life's road to uncover the real *why*s that were tormenting him.

It is an unfortunate fact that, by the time the patient has entered treatment, his addiction has often become an all-consuming problem in his life. In fact, his addiction has become his life. He has no way, at this point, to separate his addiction from the emotional problems that are causing it. But addiction cannot be successfully treated in isolation from what is *causing* it. This is where we meet the patient—at this place of grueling physical withdrawal and terrible emotional confusion—and begin the journey.

DUAL DIAGNOSIS

Dual diagnosis is a concept that emerged over twenty years ago, but it is still not well understood by the medical establishment. Simply, it is a phrase used to describe people who suffer from both an addiction and a psychiatric disorder—a "blanket" diagnosis that covers an enormously variable set of human conditions. For example, you can be addicted to drugs or alcohol or gambling—or a combination of different things. The psychiatric disorder can include schizophrenia, bipolar disorder, an eating disorder, clinical depression, borderline personality disorder, or panic disorder, among others. And within each combination, the severity of the addiction, as well as the degree of the psychiatric disorder, can vary, too. A high-functioning alcoholic can suffer from a mood disorder. A crack addict can suffer from clinical depression. A bulimic can also be bipolar. Running an algorithm of all the possible combinations would tax the most sophisticated computer programmer.

But make no mistake that it is this—the dual nature of the affliction of the vast majority of addicts—that remains largely undiagnosed and untreated and is ultimately responsible for the sky-high incidence of relapse.

One of the reasons that dual diagnoses are not well understood—or, indeed, not often given to patients—is that our health-care system is not set up to treat them. The health-care system has traditionally worked in one of two ways, neither of which offers much hope for the dual-diagnosis patient. In the first way, patients are treated for one type of disorder at a time. In many cases, this means that patients are initially assigned to a 28-day in-patient treatment program, and, when they emerge from their four-week detox, they may or may not begin extended treatment to address the underlying psychiatric problem that drove them to seek solace in alcohol or drugs or sex in the first place. Even a short lapse in time between celebrating the "completion" of a recovery program and beginning to work on the issue that drove the addiction can be tragic. It has been said, for example, that cocaine makes a person feel like a new man—and the first thing the new man wants is another line of cocaine. Emerging from detox, celebrating the powerful feeling of starting life over as a new, stronger, healthier person can easily backfire if the patient has no support in managing her new life—or in managing the old illness that remained undiagnosed but hasn't magically gone away.

In the second treatment model within our existing health-care system, patients are treated for both their addiction and their emotional problem at the same time, but a different doctor manages each aspect of their treatment. In this case, neither the doctor who is overseeing the addiction portion of treatment nor the doctor who is dealing with the emotional portion has a comprehensive picture of each patient's health. And frequently, each doctor is tentative in his or her prescriptions for fear of exacerbating the other disorder.

As we've said, neither of these models serves the patient well. Imagine, for a moment, that you are taken to the emergency room with that broken leg we mentioned earlier. The ER doctor immediately attends to your injury—examining your leg, ordering a series of X-rays, resetting the bones, and placing the limb in a cast. He then sets you up with crutches and perhaps a prescription for some pain medications and sends you on your way. All very good, right? But what if you mentioned to the doctor that the reason you broke your leg was a sudden dizzy spell that caused you to fall down the front porch steps and injure yourself? If the doctor doesn't attend to this aspect of your health (perhaps ordering a series of tests, discovering that you got dizzy because of extremely low blood pressure and then offering you options to regulate your blood pressure), you are inevitably going to get dizzy and fall again—perhaps the very moment you walk out of the ER with the cast on your leg, doing more harm to yourself in this next fall.

As your chance of taking another fall and breaking another bone would be very great if the underlying problem of your blood pressure wasn't concurrently brought under control, so an addict's chance of taking another drink or another line of cocaine or going on another food binge is inordinately high if her addiction and the underlying emotional issues that led to the addiction are not concurrently addressed.

Ideally, furthermore, the patient's total care is managed by one doctor who has a full grasp of the total picture of the patient's health. This is an important point. The ER doctor in our example was able to connect your broken leg with your dizzy spells and do something to decrease your chances of reinjuring yourself in real time. So the doctor who manages a comprehensive addiction and emotional recovery plan is in the best position to offer real-time support and solutions to enhance the potential that the patient will not reinjure himself through relapse.

One of the reasons that the rate of relapse remains so astronomical is that addiction is a recurring disorder. The patient continues to do the same things over and over again, expecting—but of course not getting—different results. This is because addiction, in its essence, has nothing to do with addiction! It has to do with trauma, with anxiety and depression and biochemical imbalances—and the addict's attempts to regulate and relieve his or her level of pain. In order to understand this concept a little better, let us spend some time answering a question that is a burning one to many of our patients and certainly to their family members: Why am *I* an addict? Why did *my loved one* manifest this disease? It's a simple question with a complex answer.

A number of dominoes have to fall into place for a person to develop an addiction. First in line is the "genetic" component. We'll talk more about this subject, including the ongoing research into the possible existence of an "alcoholism gene," in chapter 9. But for the purposes of our discussion here, even if an "addiction gene" exists and you are carrying this gene, you will not automatically become an addict. It might mean that you are genetically disposed to addiction, but it is not a foregone conclusion that you will develop an addiction. The gene, indeed, would sit dormant until it was provoked by environmental factors.

What are those environmental factors that can trigger personal addiction? Well, for example, whether an "addiction gene" is part of the equation or not, the prevalence of substance abuse that runs in families may well have a lot to do with learned behavior.

Learned behavior is, to state it simply, adopting for ourselves the conduct and habits we see in the people around us. These behaviors can include everything from the way we eat—our table manners or our preferences for food—to how we cross our legs when we sit down at the table to how we do the dishes when we're through with a meal. Did your family eat a lot of fruits and vegetables when you were a child? Then you are more likely to eat a lot of fruits and vegetables as an adult because you have learned from an early age that this is an appropriate way to eat. In contrast, did a lot of the meals on your family's table appear in fast-food paper bags? If so, you are more likely to hit the drive-through yourself because this is what you've been schooled to accept as appropriate. Did your family eat meals together at a table, or did they set up TV trays and have their meals while watching a favorite program? When they did the dishes, was it acceptable to let the pans dry overnight in the dish drainer or did your mom or dad insist that the pans be wiped with a cloth and put away as soon as they were washed? Even such a straightforward habit as where you keep the salt and pepper shakers was likely acquired as a child. Were the shakers always available on your family's table, or were they put away in the cupboard after each meal? Whichever way your mom and dad did it—and allowing for the compromises that are often necessary when blending the learned behaviors of newlyweds—it's likely that's where they'll be found in your adult home, too.

What is relevant about learned behavior, as it relates to addiction, is the way in which we have been schooled to cope with stress. How did our families—our parents, grand-parents, aunts, and uncles—and even close family friends, favorite teachers, or other adults in our sphere deal with tension release? Did your mother deal with a fight with your dad by going to bed? If so, it would not be unusual at all for you to use sleep as an escape, too. Did your grandfather relieve his everyday worries by going for a long walk or maybe going fishing to blow off steam? Then maybe you use physical exercise or a favorite activity to ward off pressure as well.

Did your dad react to a hard day at work by pouring himself a drink? Then taming anxiety with alcohol is something that you learned was the normal thing to do. The point is that the method of stress busting we witness as we grow up is the method we are most likely to copy in our own lives.

* * *

So, if the first domino of addiction is a genetic component and the second is environmental factors, such as learned behaviors, the third domino that has to fall into place for addiction to happen is *biochemical*.

Biochemistry is the study of the chemicals and chemical processes in living organisms—the cellular activities and compounds such as proteins, carbohydrates, acids, enzymes, and neurotransmitters that allow a living being to function: They regulate our heartbeat, monitor our food intake and tell us when we're hungry, and dilate our air passages so we can breathe.

These chemical components also control the speed and quality of the electrical impulses in our brains that we refer to as thinking and feeling, or intellect and emotion. The compounds that allow for these myriad—and, frankly, miraculous—functions are produced or processed within the billions of cells of our body at the molecular level thousands of times each minute in an intricately synchronized routine, rather like a very fast, very efficient assembly line. In a healthy human body, these biochemical processes occur seamlessly: A raw material is taken into the body—say, a glass of milk—and the appropriate cells react almost instantaneously to digest the milk and break it down into its component parts, sending molecules of calcium to another group of cells that need it to maintain bone density, molecules of water to another group of cells that need it to maintain blood volume, and molecules of protein to yet another group of cells charged with helping to heal a cut on the milk drinker's finger. The vitamin C in that glass of milk might go to fight oxidants, form the collagen needed for the body's connective tissue, or work with the iron in the milk, facilitating the iron's absorption so that the iron can do its job of transporting oxygen to the brain. From copper to zinc, vitamin A to vitamin K, fats to carbohydrates—the simple act of drinking a single glass of milk sets off thousands of molecular activities that impact nearly every system in the human body.

Now just suppose that, along with the beverage, our milk drinker also ate a turkey sandwich on whole-wheat bread with lettuce, tomato slices, a smear of mustard, and a side of broccoli salad. That's a nutritious lunch that triggers cells in every fiber of the diner's body to action, causing a whirlwind of molecular activity that the diner probably doesn't even notice—unless the diner has a particular sensitivity to one of the foods he has ingested. Perhaps he hasn't been eating enough yogurt or kefir and his gut flora is thus inadequate to combat the raffinose, an indigestible sugar found in cruciferous vegetables such as broccoli, cauliflower, and brussels sprouts; in that case, he'll probably burp his way through the afternoon.

Other than a few burps after broccoli, however, the vast majority of us blissfully take for granted the biochemical riot that is going on inside of us every waking and sleeping second of our lives. But what happens when our biochemistry goes awry? Some people are, for example, lactose intolerant. This means that their bodies can't efficiently break down the nutrients in dairy products such as yogurt, ice cream, and cheese; drinking a glass of milk would be an unpleasant experience, so they've learned to regulate their unique bio-chemistry by enjoying an iced tea with lunch or perhaps sub-stituting a soy- or almond-milk product.

Let us emphasize a phrase in that last sentence—*unique biochemistry*. It's critical to an understanding of addiction that we make clear how very exceptional each individual is bio-chemically. You may be lactose intolerant, while your best friend may have an allergy to chocolate, while your boss, whose favorite treat is chocolate ice cream, would go into anaphylactic shock if he ate a single peanut. The simple solu-tion you will all have come to is to avoid eating those foods that offend your body's biochemistry—that is, its ability to function in an efficient and pain-free manner. Often, unfor-tunately, the answer to regulating a person's unique biochem-istry is not so clear-cut—and the conditions that result from biochemical dysfunction are much graver than an intolerance of milk shakes and much less easily remedied than keeping your hand out of the nut bowl.

The conditions that we know commonly as psychiatric disorders are, at their cores, often the result of biochemical dysfunction. That is, the basis of these psychiatric problems can be physiological.

That's a big statement—*the basis of these psychiatric prob-lems can be physiological*. And it is one that is not yet broadly acknowledged primarily because science is still sorting out just what it is that all of the thousands of biochemical com-ponents in our bodies do—how they work and what systems they impact. Take serotonin, for example. Serotonin is just one of over a hundred neurotransmitters found in the human brain alone—and these hundred-plus neurotransmitters are just the ones that researchers have identified so far; evidence suggests that there are significantly more neurotransmitters at work in the human brain than just those we currently know about.

Serotonin is found mainly in the central nervous system, as well as in the gastrointestinal tract and in blood platelets. Scientists know that it's used by the body in a variety of ways—to regulate body temperature and to mediate gut movements and reproduction, for instance—but it is most well known in popular culture for its effect on our moods and how it contributes to our feelings of general satisfaction and happiness. We've heard it referred to as the body's "happy juice" and with reason: Researchers have shown that deficient levels of serotonin in the brain can be related to such debilitating disorders as obsessive-compulsive disorder (OCD), social phobia, and chronic depression. In fact, in many parts of the world, the class of drugs that alters human serotonin levels—and, thus, the patient's capacity to feel happiness—tops the prescription drug list.

While we will argue later in this book against the alarming tendency of physicians to too readily supply patients with prescription drugs for what is often self-diagnosed as "depression"—and for a more specific understanding of what constitutes the sort of "depression" for which drug therapy is appropriate—an adequate amount of serotonin is, without question, fundamentally essential to healthy brain chemistry. For now, let us simply address serotonin as a common human biochemical and answer the following question: How does the body manufacture it? Like bone and brain matter, digestive enzymes and insulin, and every other chemical compound in the body, serotonin is made from the fats and proteins, vitamins and minerals we ingest as food and drink. One of serotonin's primary raw materials is vitamin D. Now, as it happens, vitamin D is one of the rare raw biochemical materials that can enter the body apart from ingestion—sunshine is also a source of this critical vitamin. But between our evolution away from an agrarian way of life when much of the population spent the greater portion of their daylight hours planting and harvesting crops in the field and our contemporary—and not unreasonable—concerns about skin cancer that has us slathering the exposed portions of our bodies with sunscreen whenever we do venture outdoors, few of us get as much vitamin D from the sun as we actually need.

We are in the midst of what some medical professionals are calling a "vitamin D deficiency epidemic." Somewhere between 50 and 90 percent of Americans have substandard levels of vitamin D.[9] A lack of this nutrient has been tied to diseases such as cancer and heart disease, as well as disorders such as depression. It seems to us, then, that the "epidemic" of vitamin D deficiency and the epidemic numbers of anti-depressant prescriptions that are written worldwide go hand in hand. In an otherwise healthy person, however, supplementing the diet with a reputable brand of over-the-counter vitamin D tablets or drops should be enough to fight back against the lack and adequately restore the body's biochemical balance.

Now, when we refer to "an otherwise healthy person," we mean a patient who is neurotypical—that is, someone who processes such things as language and social behaviors and cues in a way that is generally perceived as "normal." It is indeed atypical social behaviors and habits that often signal what we conventionally diagnose as psychiatric illness. But the groundbreaking work of Candace B. Pert,[10] a pharmacologist and former section chief at the National Institutes of Health, has helped the medical community better understand the unbreakable link between a person's physiology and what we popularly refer to as "the mind." That is, the emotions we feel as anger, confusion, frustration, loneliness and despair, and even love and joy are, in reality, our perceptions of the molecular activities that happen in our bodies when we are confronted with situations that trigger biochemical reactions. When we are confronted by a large barking dog in the course of an otherwise leisurely stroll, it is the neurotransmitter epinephrine that causes our blood vessels to contract, our heart rate to increase, and our air passages to dilate—in short, all of the physical reactions we interpret as fear. When we are falling in love, the sensation of affinity that develops for that one specific other—that unique, irreplaceable, matchless human being we cannot and do not want to live without—is in part the result of the activation of the neurotransmitter oxytocin.

Emotions are then, to state it simply, *matter*—real, physical, measurable matter in the form of our body's chemical makeup. And it is not only the transient shock of fear of a barking dog or the elation of love that alters the chemical composition of our bodies.

> The fact that the word "trauma" has been used to describe both physical and mental damage has been a key part of my theory of how the molecules of emotion integrate what we feel at every level of what I've called our bodymind. As a practical matter, people have a hard time discriminating between physical and mental pain. So often we are "stuck" in an unpleasant emotional event—a trauma—from the past that is stored at every level of our nervous system and even on the cellular level—i.e., cells that are constantly becoming and renewing the nervous

system. My laboratory research has suggested that all of the senses, sight, sound, smell, taste, and touch are filtered, and memories stored, through the molecules of emotions, mostly the neuropeptides and their receptors, at every level of the bodymind.[11]

Physical or emotional trauma, then, can also induce long-lasting changes in our biochemistry and upset our natural chemical balance over the long haul. It is upon these chemical imbalances that we have laid the unfortunate and stigmatizing label "mental illness." Mental illness is a disease that happens when a person's biochemical processes are disrupted—his or her molecules of emotion set awry—through physical or emotional trauma.

But what do these molecules of "emotion" have to do with addiction? Remember that we told you several pages back that addiction has to do with trauma, the stress and anxiety that can result from it—and the addict's attempts to regulate and relieve his or her level of anxiety. It is biochemical imbalance that leads to anxiety in the first place—the anxiety of OCD, bipolar disorder, PTSD, panic disorder, stranger anxiety and social anxiety, and a whole host of other disorders, diseases, and syndromes that almost invariably predate the onset of addiction.

An untreated disease that predates an addiction will also postdate any temporary recovery unless it is addressed and treated in a holistic recovery program. Left untreated, the baseline of anxiety will remain, and the addict's attempts to again self-medicate that anxiety will inevitably resume—and the spiral of addiction will continue to spin downward as the addict's drug of choice again attacks an already ill-functioning biochemistry and exacerbates the physiological problem.

An appropriate dual diagnosis and concurrent treatment for both the addiction and its underlying disorder is the only method by which we can hope to make a dent in contemporary sky-high relapse rates.

*   *   *

As we conclude this brief section on the complex topic of biochemistry, there is one more overarching concept that we want to touch upon, and that is physiology versus psychology—or, as it has long been framed in countless debates both of the scholarly and dinner-table variety, nature versus nurture.

While it is true that there is an active interaction between biochemistry and psychological state—that is, that there is a biological predisposition to the temperament of any individual—it is the interaction between the individual (within his given temperament) and his world (his parents or significant other or other people to whom he is emotionally attached) that determines his psychology or emotional state. Let us break that down into a more easily understood equation: temperament + relationship/attachment issues + trauma or lack thereof = an individual's psychology or emotional state.

That is to say, certain disorders, such as bipolar disorder and schizophrenia, are based on biochemical and brain malfunction and imbalance. And while other emotional states can be influenced by chemical imbalance—take, for example, a phase-specific depression such as postpartum depression—the genesis is emotional in most cases. *Most often it is emotional trauma that leads to substance use and abuse.* But what constitutes emotional trauma will vary from person to person.

Interestingly, ongoing emotional trauma can affect biochemistry. A telling example is the elevated cortisol levels often found in women who have suffered abuse—cortisol being the stress hormone that triggers the fight-or-flight response. Discoveries such as these indicate that our emotional state is a two-way interaction between biology and psychology. This two-way street, then, is really the basis of the age-old debate between nature versus nurture. Volumes have been written on this subject over centuries, and the argument has yet to be resolved, but we think of this uncertainty as a positive thing. This is a debate that will always exist, and it is a debate that *should* always exist as we seek to understand why we do what we do. The art of addiction treatment is the ability to tease out the biology from the psychology, notice the parallels between a person's past and her present, graph the dots of experience and the lines of attribution, and discover why we humans behave as we do.

LOCUS OF CONTROL

The final phrase with which we want to familiarize you so that you can fully understand addiction and recovery is *locus of control*. Within the discipline of psychology, locus of control has been an important concept since Julian Rotter introduced it in the 1950s. The term refers simply to a person's perception of the core causalities in his or her life. Even more plainly, it has to do with who or what people recognize as having control of their fortunes. Do you believe that you have power over how you live, or do you believe that it is other forces— God; other, more powerful people; or some vague, unnamable fate—that determine the outcome of your actions?

To return to an earlier example, most of us learn early that it is the time we put into studying that allows us to pass our grade-school spelling tests. Given that all other factors are in alignment—the student has had ample opportunity to do his studying in a conducive environment, and he is not suffering from a medical condition that would get in the way of his learning, such as an undiagnosed hearing or vision problem— what happens when the student doesn't earn a passing grade in spite of study time? The answers—or excuses—a student will give to this question can be telling. Does the student confess that, during study time, he was distracted because he was listening to music at the same time or that he was preoccupied with getting to the end of study time because he was eager to play a video game? If so, the student is demonstrating that he understands that the power to actually pass the spelling test rests within himself—that he has an *internal control orientation*. It is, in general, considered psychologically healthy for a person to have an internal control orientation—to live life with the perception that he has some command over those things that he is capable of influencing.

If, however, the student tries to explain that he didn't pass his spelling test because the words were too hard or he doesn't like his teacher or he'd had a fight with one of his classmates on the morning of the test and, therefore, couldn't concentrate, he is demonstrating that he does not believe that he is capable of influencing the outcome of the ordinary event—that he has an *external control orientation*. He has relinquished his self-determination, self-control, or self-agency to some power outside of himself.

Now, these definitions of internal and external control orientation are broad. We don't want to promote a one-dimensional understanding of these terms. Some people have an overdeveloped internal control orientation that isn't matched by their competencies and/or they have an inflated sense of their own circle of influence. This can lead to neurosis, anxiety, and depression as their attempts to exert control don't pan out in reality. At the same time, those who have a control orientation that falls more to the external portion of the spectrum can be very relaxed and easygoing, leading the sort of lives in which they don't tend to "take things personally."

As we have already said, however, it is generally considered healthy to have a control orientation that focuses inward—to understand and define our individual circle of influence and accept responsibility for those things over which we do have power. Such a sense of inner control normally develops naturally as we mature, and it is a desirable trait to nurture in ourselves and in our children, as successful people almost always have a very highly developed sense of self-agency. As an example, it has been documented that top athletes tend to attribute mistakes, or "bad days," to factors that are within their power to influence, and, therefore, they are better able to locate and address the real causes of an off day and work to improve their performance in subsequent sporting events.[12]

In terms of treating addiction, the premise of locus of control—or attribution theory as it is also known—has a role to play in two critical arenas.

First, to whomever or whatever we assign control for a specific event or situation is often emotionally motivated. You've heard the phrase *blaming the victim*. Blaming the victim is an emotionally driven defense mechanism. In order to distance ourselves from the suffering of others, we tend to attribute their problems to their own internal failures or weaknesses. Is a friend struggling financially? If economic concerns are part of our own fears, it is soothing for us to believe that our friend's small bank balance is the result of his unfortunate personal characteristics or poor choices. Is our neighbor in the middle of a nasty divorce? It may be more comforting for us to believe that she "has terrible taste in men" than for us to look homeward at what may be our own precarious relationship. Among the most egregious—and, unfortunately, common—examples of blaming the victim is placing the culpability for a rape at the feet of the wounded party. "Look how scantily she was dressed! She was asking for it!" These ways of responding to another's unthinkable fate are really just other ways for the blamer to say, "I'm afraid that I could easily be the one who is doing the suffering."

Where we decide to place the locus of control depends on whose control we are talking about. We tend to attribute our own good fortune to the positive internal characteristics that we possess, and we place the blame for our misfortunes on forces beyond our influence. At the same time, we tend to attribute others' success to external factors—or "luck"—and their failure or misfortune to their negative internal characteristics. As it relates to addiction, there is every inclination for society to blame the victim—to attribute the addict's problems (medical, legal, personal) to her internal negative characteristics. This inclination is not only unhelpful—and it is therefore of utmost importance to disabuse the addict's family and friends of such notions in order to effect successful treatment—it is in direct opposition to where the addict places the blame.

The addict will, in almost all cases, place the blame for his disease on external forces. That is, the addict will almost always believe that forces outside of his control are the cause of his problems. This is the second arena in which the theory of locus of control is most important in recovery: In order for the addict to recover—and to *sustain recovery*—the locus of control must shift from external to internal.

By this we do not in the least mean to suggest that the addict must internalize society's generalized disdain for her "weakness." Far from it. We mean that the strength to sustain recovery can only come from the addict understanding and defining his circle of influence, from recognizing that there are factors over which he can exert authority and control, and from taking responsibility for the outcome of his actions.

The most effective way in which to regain a sense of internal control is to grasp at a very core level those events and circumstances—and biochemical imbalances—that caused the loss of control in the first place. At Creative Care, we cultivate the shift from external to internal control orientation by working with our patients to accomplish this understanding. We help them recognize and appreciate the events and circumstances that occurred in their lives prior to the onset of addiction and fostered the sense of disconnect and powerlessness that is at the root of their disease. We help them create a map that they can follow—again and again, and as often as necessary—that charts and illuminates the personal progression of addictive behavior. We help them connect the dots from the onset of their individual trauma through the downward spiral of addiction, and we help them stay connected to that trauma so that the behaviors that sprang from it become comprehensible—and can be changed from within, thus returning to the patients the internal locus of control—control over their own lives.

Four and a half months after Lewis began his treatment program at Creative Care, we sat down to talk with him in a scheduled therapy session. He had already made stunning progress, but what he said during that talk was heartening to us in terms of how Lewis was going to be able to sustain his wellness: "In my other treatment programs, I learned a lot about addiction but didn't learn a lot about myself." No one before had helped Lewis draw the map of his emotional life so that he could clearly see his behaviors in the bright and cleansing light of day. But with the map now before him, he was able to own the events and circumstances of his life—own the triggers for his maladaptive behaviors and avoid repeating them. At its most essential, this is the task of recovery—to break the repetitive nature of addiction by providing the patient with an emotional diagram that enables him to steer clear of behaviors that haven't worked for him in the past.

*   *   *

Lewis's treatment is still ongoing, as an out-patient, but he has been sober for six months as of this writing, the longest period of sobriety in his adult life. He is sober because he no longer thinks of his addiction as the cause of his disease but as the effect of trauma that predated the addiction—and he has taken control of the ways in which he is able to deal with and respond to the original trauma.

At Creative Care, we know that in order to break the hold of addiction, one cannot deal with it simplistically—that is, to address only the most obvious symptoms of the problem, like setting the bone of a patient with a broken leg. We want to know why that leg is broken—what is behind the observable injury. Getting to the root problem is the only way that real healing can begin—and that the prevention of future harm is possible.

CHAPTER 2

❦

The First Dot

WHERE IT HURTS

In spite of fourteen years of escalating dependency on marijuana, cocaine, and opiates—and ten of those years in the
dangerous world of drug dealing—Kevin was still a rather
youthful-looking twenty-seven-year-old. In fact, had some
Hollywood director wanted to romanticize the life and hard
times of a rising young drug kingpin, he would have done
well to cast handsome Kevin—with his mop of curly black
hair and intense, dark eyes—in the role. But real life, as we all
know, is nothing like the movies. Kevin had the good looks
and the wads of cash to act the part he most craved—
"player"—but he rarely got the girl. There was something off
about his posture and his gait, a certain jerky clumsiness, that
put women off—and that easily betrayed to us, as therapists,
the breadth of his problems. By the time a patient arrives at
Creative Care, we already have a fairly in-depth history of
the personal difficulties he has faced along his life's trajectory, so that even in the initial clinical interview, we have a
strong working knowledge of his problems and their origins.
But even to a layperson, it's obvious that one cannot spend
ten years as a drug dealer and walk away without a lot of
emotional issues.

Like most of our patients, however, Kevin was, at the
outset of his treatment, in strong denial of his issues and
the connection between those issues, his emotions, and the
resulting behaviors he exhibited. Denial, let us immediately
point out, does not necessarily equal reticence or any hesi-
tancy to talk to us. Frequently, a patient will come to us and

in the first clinical interview, will report the most profound traumatic history. She will go into great detail to describe ordeals that are, to most people, unthinkable. In her reporting, though, there will be, at this stage, very little genuine emotion or connection to the pain of the trauma and how that trauma has affected her life and led to her self-medication and addiction.

Kevin, in contrast, would admit only to feeling "depressed."

Depression, these days, is an enormously misunderstood malady. Many people who are feeling genuinely sad—and for a genuinely reasonable cause: They have lost their girlfriend or their job or have experienced the recent death of a loved one—will self-diagnose as "depressed." These people do not understand "depression" beyond the oft-used societal catchall term. Depression is a real disorder with a real definition. It is a feeling of hopelessness, helplessness, and worthlessness that continues for at least two weeks and prevents a person from functioning at his normal capacity. According to the *Diagnostic and Statistical Manual of Mental Disorders (DSM-IV)*, a manual published by the American Psychiatric Association to aid clinicians in the diagnosis of disease, when a person suffers from at least five of the following nine symptoms *at the same time*, he may be more than simply sad and would do well to seek help for what is a treatable medical condition:

- a dejected mood that can last for most of the day but is often most intense in the morning
- a daily sense of fatigue or lack of energy
- daily struggles with feelings of guilt and insignificance
- an inability to concentrate or make decisions

- insomnia or hypersomnia, which is excessive sleep-ing, that occurs nearly every day
- a noticeable or extended disinterest in activities that were once pleasurable
- recurring thoughts about dying, or even suicide, but notably *not* the fear of death, which is, to some greater or lesser degree, a normal human concern that nearly all people face
- a sense of restlessness, which is known as psycho-motor agitation, or a sense of being slowed down, which is known as retardation
- a noteworthy change in weight—a gain or a loss of more than 5 percent within a one-month period

It has been anecdotally estimated that at any given time, up to a quarter of the U.S. population will say that they are suf-fering from varying degrees of depression. But in reality, according to the National Institute of Mental Health (NIMH), about 14.8 million American adults[1]—or a little less than 7 percent of the population—are truly afflicted with clinical or major depression.

This is not to say, as we pointed out, that genuine sad-ness does not exist, and with good cause, or that the peo-ple who find themselves enduring a temporary bout of it should not seek professional help to alleviate their gloom. What is tragic is that antidepressants such as Zoloft and Paxil have become so prevalent and prescriptions for these drugs so commonplace. The experience of sadness is part of the human condition, and the human condition cannot be medicated away. While research has shown that medica-tion can indeed be helpful in treating clinical depression, simply prescribing a pill does not remedy the depressed state but merely masks the symptoms of it. When a pill is the only treatment offered for despair, this is, in effect, consigning the patient to a life of artificial, chemical happiness and ignorance about his or her authentic life condition. Think of it in this way: One morning, over your first cup of coffee, you look up and happen to notice that the paint in a corner of the kitchen ceiling—just below where your bathtub is located on the second floor—is beginning to flake and discolor. You could respond to this observation by getting out your ladder, scraping away the peeling paint, spackling over the rough spot on the plaster, and putting on a fresh coat of paint. The corner would look brand new again, at least for a matter of hours or even days, but most people wouldn't think much of this solution. They would realize that the slow leak that caused the flaking and discoloration in the first place is going to ruin any handiwork they attempt if they don't get the plumbing behind the plaster fixed. The same is the case with depression. Although a plethora of pharmaceutical-industry television commercials and magazine ads would have you believe otherwise, it is *talking* through the despair—from the mildest sadness to bona fide clinical depression—that is the most helpful way to alleviate and eliminate the root cause of the pain.

This is not to say that antidepressant drugs don't have their place. Often a short course of this class of drugs *combined* with talk therapy can do the most good. That is, the pharmaceuticals can serve to lighten the symptoms of depression so that the patient can more readily do the work with his or her therapist to uncover the root cause of the problem. Moreover, masking the depression with medication and not exploring what led to the depression dooms the patient to recurring bouts of the disorder. The blessing and curse of the human condition is that what ails us will continue to present itself until we resolve it—until we *heal* it.

To understand why getting to the root cause is so critical in healing depression, it is necessary to go far beyond the catchall meaning of the word—to understand that the insomnia, fatigue, and other frequently debilitating troubles that we normally associate with depression are indeed just the *symptoms* of the condition. In reality, depression is not about sadness—it is in most cases about anger.

Depression frequently is internalized anger or anger turned inward. A clinically depressed person is most often someone who is sitting on a great deal of rage—to the point that when a patient self-diagnoses with depression, the first reasonable clinical question to ask is: What pissed you off?

As we've already pointed out in chapter 1, addiction and anxiety go hand in hand—and anxiety and depression are cousins. Their common denominator is resentment. Depending on the dynamics that are part of any individual patient's background—the sort of trauma that was endured, the family culture, and the way that stress relief was modeled in the home—anger has been turned off to some degree and remains unexpressed. But the anger doesn't go away simply because there is no outlet to express it. It is turned inward. Remember Lewis from chapter 1? "Just call me 'the Titanic!'" he cheerfully informed us when we first met him. A competent clinician will recognize Lewis's sad attempt at humor as a sign of how disconnected the patient is from his own emotions. Lewis had done a 180-degree turn away from anger, disavowing his resentment with a joke and making himself the butt of it. Meanwhile, however, he was roiling inside. And the only way to calm anger that is boiling out of sight is to help the patient identify the cause of it and help the patient make sense of it.

But lame jokes, however heartbreaking, aren't the worst of depression, of course. There is also real danger associated with containing and masking unidentified anger. Depression becomes more serious as the resentment is left unexpressed because then it gets dammed up. It turns into anxiety. It escalates. It manifests in panic or anxiety attacks. It manifests as attention deficit disorder (ADD) or as heightened paranoia. It spirals into psychosis, a complete departure from a reality that the patient can no longer handle, process, or channel into a truth he can make sense of—a break that is, at a very organic level, the brain protecting itself from blowing a fuse. It's a temporary protective mechanism that prevents the ultimate angry gestures: murder or suicide.

Kevin's initial admission that he felt "depressed" was, in many ways, a heartening sign. Although he was using the word in relation to the superficial, catchall meaning, we now had a way in—a starting point to help guide him toward understanding a new definition of depression and to identify those things that had made him so very mad.

*   *   *

Often, but not always, when a patient first arrives for treatment, there are, in addition to emotional issues, physical issues—especially concerning withdrawal—that must be attended to immediately. If the addiction is, for example, to sex or to gambling, there is no physiological detox period. In Kevin's case, he needed to detoxify his body from the effects of cocaine, which was the drug he'd indulged in most frequently, and other illegal substances. Although this might seem counterintuitive, there is really not a great deal of physiological detoxification associated with the cessation of cocaine use. The effects of depriving the body of cocaine once it has become used to the substance are mostly emotional—the patient becomes extremely paranoid.

But detoxing from the use of cocaine was nothing new to Kevin. Just prior to arriving at Creative Care, he'd spent fourteen days in another in-patient treatment center, although it was not a dual-diagnosis facility; Kevin's family, and even to some extent Kevin himself, knew that his needs were not being fully met. When he arrived, he was still in the grip of lingering paranoia, and his anxiety level was high.

Further complicating how we would proceed with Kevin's physical stabilization was the imperative that, before we could delve into the psychological potential of real depression, we needed to rule out any possible biological cause for it. It is widely agreed upon in both the medical and psychological communities that, before a diagnosis of a psychological disorder can be truly assigned, any medical issues that might be causing the problem must be ruled out. The symptoms of depression are frequently experienced on a physical level—lack of energy, sleeplessness or other sleep problems, loss of appetite—but that doesn't mean that the genesis of the disorder is physical. Psychological issues frequently do produce physical symptoms.

Moreover, research indicates a real biological link with depression. It has been found, for example, that there is a correlation between maternal depression and long-term depression in the adult children of these mothers.[2] It was found that if an infant or a young child had a profoundly depressed mother and that depressed mother was the primary caregiver, then the child was also likely to suffer from depression.

This was thought to occur because the centers of the brain that are responsible for elation or joy were not stimulated in the mother/child relationship and so this part of the child's brain was not normally developed. Further, it was discovered that if this part of the brain was not sufficiently stimulated in childhood, the individual was unable to develop the capacity for joy later in life. In these cases, it was clear that the mother's depression affected her child's neurological development. Can we conclude from this study that depression is biological? Perhaps on some level. But it is important to note that in these cases, there was no antidepressant medication that, with long-term use, proved successful on the individual study participants.

*   *   *

Still, in Kevin's case, we decided that a short course of antidepressant medication would be helpful to him in dealing with the paranoia and anxiety and in getting the most out of his talk-therapy sessions.

Why did we choose an antidepressant over an antianxiety drug? Antianxiety drugs are, historically, meant for short-term use, after all, and that was what we had in mind. But, while antianxiety medications do act as sedatives, they are also narcotics—and that means that in and of themselves they are addictive. And the addict's brain reacts in the same way whether the drug is an illegal or a prescription one: The patient is sedated, but he is at the same time still experiencing life behind the mask of an accustomed narcotic buzz. Antidepressant medications, in contrast, are not narcotics. They can be used for a longer period, if necessary, because they are not in and of themselves addictive. The patient feels the relief that the antidepressant offers through its positive effect on his biochemical makeup while at the same time not simply becoming addicted to a legal drug.

This relief can be crucial as the patient's therapy begins, so he can face the hard task of identifying the trauma or traumas that have impacted his life with a clearer head and in a more stable frame of mind. As we have already said, most patients begin the initial clinical sessions appallingly detached from their emotions. The gap between their life stories and how they relate those stories to us can feel like an abyss. One of our patients, for example, went into minute and graphic detail about the incest she had suffered for years at the hands of an older stepbrother, but her affect was so flat and out of context with her distressing story that she may as well have been telling us how to take apart the engine of a 747 and put it back together. To be sure, some patients are well aware of the shock value of the tales they have to tell, relating the details to us in order to gauge our reactions or to see if they can get a rise out of the new therapist. But even these patients who are conscious of the more lurid aspects of their stories don't *feel* the associated emotions that are generally considered appropriate. They can tell us stories of unimaginable pain, and yet the way in which they narrate their story reflects that they are experiencing no pain—no resentment, no anger, no guilt, no regret, no emotional connection whatsoever to what has been experienced.

Just as often, if not more so, however, the patient reacts to his initial clinical sessions with a phobic response. A phobic response is defined as an intense but irrational, uncontrollable, persistent fear in which the sufferer will go to great lengths to avoid being in the situation or coming into contact with the object that provokes this response. The severity of phobic responses has a wide range—from mild repulsion to outright terror—and many people can function quite efficiently even while their phobias are active. Indeed, anywhere from 5 to 9 percent[3] of people in America alone deal with some sort of phobia at any given time: The fear of flying, closed-in spaces, bridges, heights, water, or specific animals such as barking dogs are all common. We've heard of and/or treated patients whose phobias involve rather more personalized objects or activities: dead birds or raw eggs, walking down a set of stairs, or eating from a plate that has a decorative pattern on its surface. The celebrity Billy Bob Thornton has gone public with his very real but nondebilitating fear of antiques.

For an addict, the phobic response is related to his or her past—to reliving and retelling the traumas they have experienced. They don't want to do it.

Have you ever heard someone say something on the order of, "Don't go there," when you bring up a certain touchy subject of conversation? Perhaps your spouse doesn't want to discuss a situation in which she or he was unintentionally insensitive because it is embarrassing for her or him to recount. Maybe a friend is rebuffing your romantic advice as gently as she can because she doesn't want to hear again that she has poor taste in men; she's telling you that she already knows your opinion. You may have even caught yourself saying something like this to your mother if you've ever complained to her about a child's misbehavior and she responds by reminding you that you yourself were a handful when you were growing up. In each of these cases, the "don't go there" response is relatively mild, the reaction provoked because the person has a clear and often disconcerting memory of both the events as well as their subsequent behaviors.

In contrast, for the addict, it is often a matter of "can't go there." That is, the patient truly cannot either put her finger on the event or events that were painful or is so emotionally closed down that she can't relate to the event as painful. The patient has been spackling over the slow leak in her psyche for so long—self-medicating the psychic wound with her addiction for so long—that she can no longer recognize it for the wound that it is.

For these patients, there is often a great deal of frustration in that they cannot identify a clear trauma. Rather, what they express is a prevailing if generalized feeling of hurt and pain. For us as clinicians, uncovering the raw spot at the heart of the generalized ache is crucial to successful treatment. Let's revisit the broken leg we spoke of in chapter 1, and let's assume for the purposes of this example that the break was clean and noncompound—that is, the sort of break that impacts the bone but doesn't break the skin. There may be a bruise or some swelling, but those relatively minor results of the break are well hidden under a pair of slacks, and there is no obvious evidence of injury. In this case, if you, as the patient, are unable or unwilling to communicate to the emergency-room doctor "where it hurts," the doctor may have to spend a lot of time examining and X-raying your head, your arms, or your rib cage before he is able to locate the tender spot and begin the healing process.

With patients who exhibit a phobic response to revisiting their traumas, we are, stated very simply, trying to find out "where it hurts." How do we do that?

First of all, if it's appropriate for the patient, pharmaceuticals can sometimes help in this initial phase. While there are no medications that specifically treat phobic response—there is no pill anyone can take to overcome a fear of heights or a dislike of aggressive dogs—antidepressants, such as those we prescribed for Kevin, can often reduce the anxiety associated with a phobic response to the point where the patient is more comfortable and amenable and simply *able* to begin sorting out the source of his pain.

Much more important, however, is the continued reassurance of a dedicated therapist. This sounds very basic, but it is fundamental to building a base from which the individual patient is able to begin to tolerate the pain of telling his story and connecting to his pain. In each session, we simply, again and again, let the patient know that we are there, patiently waiting to help him figure it out—to help him awaken to the emotional import of what occurred in his life. As we have already said, it is frequently the case that the individual has lived with painful memories for so long that she is unable to generate any feeling around the events. It takes time and patience to help her get to a genuine connection to the emotions underlying her personal history; it takes a sense of safety and trust—and trust, of course, takes time to flourish. One of the most frequent things that we say to a patient is, "It's OK. I will wait; I will be here when you are ready. If this were easy, you and I wouldn't be here."

It's important here to stress a point that some readers may find contrary. Many people, and most societies, look upon the disease of addiction as a "weakness"—as the personal failure of the addict. This couldn't be further from the truth. It takes a great deal of strength to go through treatment. This is one of the reasons that addiction treatment is so hard—and that so often, without proper treatment of all aspects of the patient's condition, relapse happens. The addiction itself is tough, and the issues that brought the person to addiction are also tough, so the patient is in essence experiencing two grave discomforts in one: He is relinquishing the self-medication that has for so long enabled him to bear his pain and at the same time delving into the pain at its most basic level—a double whammy that could bring the most mentally healthy to their knees.

*   *   *

Like most patients, when Kevin began to feel safe in our care, he began to recall and to open up more and more about the circumstances and events that had led him to seek solace in drugs. We found out that he had a complicated relationship with his father, who was an active alcoholic; because of the alcoholism, Kevin's relationship with his dad had been erratic for most of his life, but Kevin was dependent on his father to care for his beloved dogs while he was in treatment. We found out that his relationship with his mother was similarly complicated: After she had divorced Kevin's dad, she had insisted on sleeping in the same bed as Kevin until he was well into his teens. We found that, in spite of Kevin's presentation of himself as a "player," he actually had a steady girlfriend—and he was terrified of her because she would beat him to a pulp whenever she was annoyed with him. We found out that Kevin had had a series of motorcycle accidents— one of them profound enough to have possibly caused a brain injury that exacerbated his chemical dependencies. We found out that Kevin had a little brother to whom he was devoted—and that, in his addictive dysfunction, this devotion had led him to set his little brother up in the drug business; the guilt he experienced, and was eventually able to express, over this terribly misguided career guidance was intense.

Through the months that it took for Kevin to recall and become comfortable in telling his story, we let him know every day that we were there to meet him where he was—to walk with him and to stop along the way as he needed. Through this process of walking and walking again the path of the patient's life, we were helping him to make sense of the trajectory of pain and traumas that he had experienced, to establish what event or relationship represented the first ache, the first emotional wound—the first dot. In Kevin's case, it was the erratic, insecure, and conditional relationship he had experienced with his father—a relationship in which escape through alcohol had been the model for stress relief.

But what was the next dot on the map of Kevin's life? What was the next place where he had to stop and take account? Continuity often presents a problem for our patients. They will begin to vary the sequence of their story and jump from one dot to another in the confusion and fog of their general pain. Our goal is to help them understand why they are skipping or mixing up not only parts of their story but the pain attendant in any specific portion of it. We can then gently lead them back to the start again. As an example, Kevin was able to connect in relatively short order with the anger he felt at his girlfriend for the physical pain and injury she had caused him. It was an accomplishment, certainly, that he was able to attach emotions to this relationship. But this was not where the root of his anger resided. His relationship with his girlfriend, we were clear by this point even if Kevin was not yet himself, was perhaps dot 14 on the map of his life—she was Fort Wayne, so to speak, and we were able to reorient him and help guide him back to Toledo to spend some time in that prior place of his life, integrating and resolving the traumas that had come before he had ever met his girlfriend.

It's not unusual for a patient to pick a dot in the middle of his trajectory, latch onto it, and then zigzag all over the map.

The story is inconsistent and muddled. But when the story is inconsistent and muddled, so are the patient's emotional connections. It's not unusual, either, that the patient is unaware of how out of control his thought progressions are during the whole process—unaware that he has aimed for Fort Wayne by way of Albuquerque, so, of course, he is struggling to get to his destination.

The patient may, in fact, be reluctant or ambivalent about getting to his destination at all. Remember Lewis from chapter 1? Part of Lewis's treatment was necessarily helping him to come to grips with the reason that he maintained his extraordinary weight. As with all addictions—and make no mistake, overeating to the point of obesity is indeed an addiction to food—the reason for the problem is multifaceted and often difficult to pinpoint. But the first time we broached the problem of his weight with Lewis, he immediately became silent and withdrawn. We recognized that Lewis was not ready to address this facet of his addiction—and we understood why: If Lewis were no longer to have the insulating layer of fat on his body, he would also no longer have one of the insulations from life that he had grown to depend on. If he were in good physical health, he would be asked to participate in life in a different—and, for Lewis, an unfamiliar and therefore scary—way.

Further, by taking control of his weight and his health, Lewis would be doing a thing that was, for him, completely out of character: He would be putting himself—his health and his well-being—first. And addicts, in a very general but foundational sense, are constitutionally unable to put themselves first. They have spent their lives avoiding putting themselves first, hiding themselves and their problems behind habitual and destructive behaviors.

In Kevin's case, discovering the basis for his depression and healing from it would mean that he would no longer experience his life in the same destructive but comfortable way. But by walking the path of the patient's life with him again and again and as many times as it takes, the dots inevitably become a well-worn path—and a less scary one as well. With ongoing treatment, we are seeking to make the connections so understood that there is almost a groove where the dots connect from point to point. In this way, the patient will be able to know for himself where he has strayed from the path and be able to double back and reright himself when he is lost. This is the process of returning to the patient his locus of control, his ability to understand where his behaviors originate, so that he will recognize his influence over them—and be well equipped to exert his influence to change them.

And this—the patient's ability to exert self-contained influence to make healthy changes and choices—is the key to not merely temporary recovery but to the prevention of relapse.

CHAPTER 3

A Fork in the Road

WHEN DREW ARRIVED at Creative Care, he was eighteen years old and mad at everyone—primarily his mother. For most of his life, Drew's mother had found ways to excuse his increasingly erratic behaviors. From the time that he was fourteen and was first caught smoking marijuana, Drew's mother had eagerly believed each of his promises that he wouldn't do drugs ever again *this time*. The first time she'd found a green glass bong in his bedroom, she was glad to accept Drew's explanation that he was just "holding on to it for a friend." The first time he had stolen to get drug money—by breaking into a neighbor's car in his family's upscale suburban enclave—his mother had provided him with an alibi because she was terrified of her son being taken to jail.

Now, for a reason that seemed to Drew to be drawn from out of the blue, she had put her foot down. Either he stopped using drugs—not to mention got his sticky fingers under control—or she was through with him. It wasn't that she didn't love him—quite the contrary. She was panicked every time he disappeared and wouldn't answer his cell phone for days at a time. She was shattered anew each time the police called her to report that her son was being held for committing yet another petty crime. She was sleepless and exhausted with worry about his deteriorating potential—he was a naturally bright young man, but he had barely made it through high school; now, he demonstrated no interest in planning for his future beyond hanging out with a questionable crowd of his high school friends in a run-down apartment one of them had rented in the nearby city. She loved

Drew so much that it had simply become unbearable to be a part of his life.

It was from Drew's other family members—his grand-mothers, his aunts, his siblings—however, that we found quick confirmation of our suspicion that the threat Drew's mother was making was a desperate but idle one. Drew's problematic behaviors had not, of course, begun in one giant conflagration in his fourteenth year but were part of an escalating pattern of defiance from early childhood. Drew had already been in and out of the principal's office, juvenile hall, and several other residential facilities by the time he came to us. In the fifth grade, Drew had bullied his teacher so unmercifully that he had actually brought her to tears—and his mom had placed the blame for the bullying on the teacher's incompetence. When he was in the sixth grade, his mom had noticed that none of his usual gang of friends was coming around after school and looking for him to play—and she had accepted unquestioningly Drew's explanation for the defection, that those old friends were all "losers," even going so far as to drive him the quarter of a mile to school each day so he wouldn't have to walk alone, snubbed. In the seventh grade, Drew hit his mother for the first time. It was an incident that had understandably outraged his extended family. His mom had been quick to reassure them that Drew hadn't really hurt her and that he had apologized profusely immediately afterward, but this was when they had begun to subtly distance themselves from him.

"I can't even look at him," one of his grandmothers told us sorrowfully. "He's my grandson, and he disgusts me."

Although Drew had willingly agreed to allow us to talk with the members of his extended family, understanding on some gut level that these people were now a crucial part of his recovery, it was clear that he was irritated and resentful of them, too. Unlike his mother, they would no longer accept or believe in his apologies. Part of his anger in this could be seen as justifiable: He *was* truly remorseful after each outburst or disruptive incident, his apologies sincere, and his intentions to get his life back on track heartfelt. Beneath his frightening behaviors was a fierce, if unfocused, intelligence, as well as an acute need to be loved that caused him to be mortified, always in retrospect, by the things he did when he was not in control of himself. At these times, he would be desperate for forgiveness and, according to his extended family, able to spend days or even weeks "posing" as a model son; they were fearful now that, after a few days or even a week in treatment posing as a "model patient," he would appeal to his mother to "spring" him—and that she would, once again, take his side and acquiesce. His mom's misguided forgiveness—her "soft spot"—was likely to be the unintentionally weak link in Drew's recovery.

It is essential to know that while we, as clinicians and treatment providers, may understand how life events con- nect with emotions and behaviors, it is only truly meaningful to the patients when they are able to make those connec- tions for themselves. Lewis needed to be able to take him- self back to his own personal first dot—the place in his life when the longing for escape through food, alcohol, and ulti- mately prescription medications began to be overwhelming for him. Kevin needed to be able to take himself back to his own personal starting point—the crisis that precipitated his fall into opiate use. Drew needed to find the first fault line of his enormous anger and the rebellion that it engendered. It is only with this ability to map the origins of their own needs that they would be able to learn to cope with the emotions that triggered their addictions and to replace their negative reactions and habits with healthier ones.

This process of freeing oneself from the clutches of addiction is by necessity a collaborative one. Without a skilled therapist who can help the patient discover and articulate the past trauma or traumas that inform her current behaviors, and guide her back there again and again to reconcile the formative events, the patient is unlikely to break free of the confusion and conflicting emotions that cause her to desire to flee once more into addiction.

But patient and therapist are not the only two entities involved in a successful recovery—not by a long shot. The process of recovery is one that is almost always fraught with the push and pull of warring factions, not only within the patient herself, but also with the people within the patient's life.

*   *   *

Enabling is a word with conflicting meanings. To enable means to allow, to facilitate, to permit, to make possible, to provide somebody with the means to make something happen. Viewed in one way, the connotations are all positive. Because your mother and father made wise financial decisions and not a few personal sacrifices along the way, you were able to go to the college of your choice. Because your boss gave you the go-ahead to work on that new marketing idea you had, you were able to save your company a substantial amount of advertising dollars and earn a promotion. Because you made the effort to drive your daughter to dance class two evenings a week, she now has a starring role in her high school's seasonal production of *The Nutcracker*.

But *enabling* has another, darker meaning. When the word is used in connection with difficult or unacceptable behaviors, it refers to dysfunctional approaches to problem solving—to actions and attitudes that are in all likelihood well intentioned but that, in fact, serve only to perpetuate the problem. An example of this phenomenon is the unfortunately classic situation of the spouse who covers for an alcoholic by calling him in sick to work when he is hung over, making excuses to friends or family for the alcoholic's inappropriate behaviors, and generally making sure that the alcoholic is not held accountable for the harm he inflicts when his judgment is impaired.

The spouse in this case, in psychological terms, would be referred to as codependent—that is, someone who has the tendency to go overboard in caring for a loved one and/or to be overly passive about situations that negatively affect his own life. Codependency does not, we want to take care to point out, refer to normal caretaking. Parents, for example, are expected to give high priority to their children, and they are likely to want to make certain sacrifices on their child's behalf. Helping a child with homework, coaching his baseball team, and driving her to dance lessons are activities that are *empowering*. What is the difference between empowering and enabling? Here is a quick litmus test you can take if you are ever unsure of how your own actions might be interpreted by someone you are trying to help: Empowering someone is doing something for someone or helping him to do something that he does not have the capacity to do himself; enabling is doing something for someone that she can do, or very well ought to be doing, for herself.

But enablers find it very hard to believe that anyone else can perform a task as well as they can do it themselves. They have a strong and often quite sincere desire to lend a hand, but then they become anxious or upset when the people they are trying to help don't follow their advice. It's easier for enablers to take control of a situation rather than delegate, and because of this, they frequently take on more responsibilities than any one person could reasonably handle. They are usually under a great deal of stress and poor at time management, and they will shove their own needs aside in order to keep the multiple commitments they make to others. But people who neglect their own needs, both physical and emotional, to an unhealthy level are, in reality, setting themselves up to run into physical and psychological health problems down the road themselves. And parents who neglect their own needs may be less effective at raising healthy children and may, in fact, do their children harm.

Shielding someone from the consequences of his or her actions is, to put it plainly, a way of causing harm. The trials we encounter in life serve a purpose. They are opportunities to develop judgment and to grow emotionally. If, for example, Drew had been held accountable for making his grade-school teacher cry, it might have helped him to develop a more profound sense of empathy for the suffering of others and/or the respect for authority figures that could have precluded his physical attack on his mother. As it was, he was allowed to walk away from the incident with no consequences—and the lesson he learned was that he could get away with being a bully and his mother would take his side and see that he was not punished, even if he had to bully *her*, too. In fact, this was part of the story of Drew's entire young life: He could go whistling along without care on his destructive path and his mother would always be there, cleaning up after his every mistake.

In not allowing her child to "face the music" for his mistakes, Drew's mother was denying him the opportunity to build the skill sets that would better serve him in all the relationships he would have throughout his life. Even further, the codependent parent or spouse, friend or coworker denies the addict the opportunity and the motivation to become well, as there is no urgency to take responsibility for an addiction or the actions that result from it when all of the problems it creates are "solved" by an enabler.

Enabling is a major factor in the perpetuation of addiction. Think of it this way: If eating a quart of chocolate ice cream a day didn't contribute to heart disease, diabetes, and the expansion of our thighs, a great many of us would likely be eating more of it than we already do. If an addict is continually bailed out of the blame for damage left in the wake of his addictive behaviors, from where will the motivation come to clean up those bad behaviors?

By the time patients come to us, their addiction has in all likelihood led them to a place where their life is no longer intact. They have frequently burned bridges and left scores of relationships in the dust. But typically—and very cannily—addicts are able to surround themselves with people who enable their addictive behaviors. Although there may well be a professed desire for the patient to recover and become clean and sober, there are strong forces at work to inhibit and sometimes even sabotage the successful outcome for the patient.

Frequently, the people in the addict's life are not even aware of the impact of their own behaviors and how they dovetail with the addict's. Therefore, it becomes a very important part—even an essential part—of treatment to have both the patient and the patient's significant others aware of the interplay of issues for both the addict and themselves. If you have a loved one who is suffering from an addiction, here are some questions you can ask yourself to find out if you have been helping to enable them to continue their self-destructive lifestyles:

- Do I find myself continually making excuses for my loved one's unacceptable behaviors or bad judgment? Have I ever called someone's boss and told her that he had the flu when he was really just hung over? Have I ever dismissed my teenager's drug use as "just a phase"? Have I ever withheld the truth from a teacher, a friend, or the police in order to cover for a loved one's mistake?

- Do I take responsibility for tasks my loved one is, or should be capable of, performing himself? Have I ever routinely done laundry for an adult child? Cleaned his apartment? Paid her bills?

- Have I ever held my tongue in order to avoid an argument? Do I keep my opinions to myself because I fear my spouse or my child will love me less, or even leave me, if I speak up—or because I fear emotional and/or physical reprisal? Do I feel a sense of guilt when I do assert myself?

- Does my loved one belittle me or threaten me physically if I don't immediately acquiesce to his needs? Do I routinely ignore or excuse this abusive behavior?

- Do I find more often than not that I don't have time to perform all the obligations I have taken on? Do I find myself becoming angry at my inability to manage my time, or do I experience an almost chronic anger that my loved ones don't appreciate all that I sacrifice on their behalf?

- Am I more invested in the needs of others than I am in what I myself might want? Have I ever done something just to keep the peace even though I didn't want to do it? Have I ever cooked a special meal because someone in the family didn't like what I happened to be serving for dinner? Have I ever skipped an activity I might have enjoyed because my child wanted me to chauffeur her to the mall or my spouse didn't feel like going with me? Have I ever participated in sex when I didn't want to?

- Have I ever identified myself, even just *to* myself, as a "people pleaser"? As "patient as a saint"? A "victim"? Do I have difficulty identifying my own emotions and communicating them to others? Do I minimize my emotions? Do my emotions sometimes take me by surprise so that an emotional explosion ensues?

Now, almost all of us have helped out a friend or a family member in dire circumstances. When your sister calls because she's stranded with a flat tire and needs a ride to work *right now*, if it is at all within your power, you'll likely jump right in the car and help her out. That's what sisters and brothers are for, right? The determining factors between empowering and enabling are the degree of the help that is sought and how the recipient responds to your assistance. If there is an expectation of assistance and there is no expression of appreciation for it, or if the occasional help has become a habit, then it is time to assess the norm of the relationship. In short, if you can't answer the question, What do *I* want? with clarity and then act on it with confidence, it's very possible that you will want to reevaluate your relationship to your loved one and to your loved one's addiction. In doing so, you will increase the patient's chances of achieving a durable sobriety—and improve the quality of both of your lives in the process.

Long-term recovery and relapse prevention requires, as you can see, more than one-on-one collaboration with a dedicated therapist. A patient may successfully complete twenty-eight days, three months, or a year or longer in a supportive residential treatment program, but lasting sobriety is very difficult to achieve if the patient returns to a home situation that hasn't been concurrently healed and in which a stable, responsible sort of support isn't available.

How does one go about breaking the habit of enabling? The first step is to acknowledge that it's not an easy job. The fact is that much of the time, enabling happens because of the affection that the enabler genuinely feels for the patient. The desire to "make her life easier" may be misguided, but it is well intentioned. Breaking the habit of enabling requires that the enablers experience a shift in how they define and act upon the foundational human feeling of love. That's a tall order, and we suggest taking it in small, achievable steps.

At Creative Care, just as at almost all residential treatment facilities, we impose a time of limited interaction with the outside world when a patient initially enters our care. During this period, the patient's contact with friends and family is restricted, if not precluded altogether. This period typically lasts from two to eight weeks, and it serves dual purposes. It is an important time for the patient, when she can focus exclusively on her own healing, free from distractions. No excuses need be made, no relationships negotiated;

the patient's sole responsibility is centered on stabilizing her physical and emotional health for the hard work of core recovery that lies ahead.

But this period is also a time that can help break the cycle of enabling—for both the patient and those who have been enabling him. The trained therapists the patient encounters will gently but consistently hold him accountable for his daily behavior in the rehabilitation facility. Back home, his friends and family are encouraged to use this time to reevaluate their own behaviors and to start the shift toward a more wholesome way of supporting and loving the patient upon his own return. During this time when contact is curtailed, or precluded altogether, we learn a great deal about not only the dynamics of the patient but also the dynamics of the family, friends, and others significant in the patient's life. It is very helpful to the therapist to learn who does what, whom it's done to, and how it's done when they are not allowed access to the patient. As we work with the patient in this initial phase, without outside involvement, we gather a greater sense of her obstacles to recovery. Then, when the patient is again allowed to be in contact with those outside of treatment, the contact is discussed in advance, and potential stumbling blocks are presented and ways to avoid them proposed and processed. A "debriefing" occurs after the outside contact, as it is entirely possible—indeed, frequently likely—that these initial contacts with family and friends outside of the therapeutic community will set the patient back a few dots—but the setbacks in these cases are not always negative events. Being set back can be, with the help of a trained therapist as a guide, a time in which the patient can learn—a time in which he can come to an understanding and recognition of the role each personal relationship has played in his life and may play out in the future. This relationship review can lead to a heightened level of awareness that will serve the patient well in terms of relapse prevention. In the best of circumstances, then, the therapist works with both patients and their loved ones to bring into the light of day the dynamics of the relationships.

There is no "one way" to accomplish this shift toward more wholesome personal relationships. Often, a combination of the suggestions we offer in what follows is most effective. But healthy reintegration into the family and the larger society is the ultimate goal, so it is almost always essential that the patient's family members take stock of their own behaviors and realize the importance of making changes in their own attitudes and actions—and the profound impact these efforts can have in helping the patient sustain her recovery. To this end, and after any initial holding period, we promote regular communication between the patient and family members through letters, telephone calls, and visits.

Suggestions for the work a patient's friends and family members can do outside of supportive communication include the following:

- Work one on one with a qualified therapist to address and correct enabling tendencies.
- Find a support group and attend meetings regularly—there are many twelve-step programs, such as those offered by Al-Anon and Alateen, that focus on codependency issues.
- Read books that can help explain and clarify enabling—many times, it is merely seeing our own experience reflected in the stories of others that will cause the light bulb to go off and habits to

begin to change. A list of our favorite recommen-
dations follows in the bibliography at the end of
this book.

At the end of the day, however, there are two tools that
are basic—very nearly indispensable—to anyone who is
committed to discarding the habit of enabling. The first is
continual and careful self-monitoring. It is developing the
habit of asking ourselves, Why am I doing this? Is this what I
really want to do? Is this something that my loved one should,
by all rights, be doing for himself? Journaling can be a very
helpful way to facilitate a growing sense of self-awareness of
how our actions impact the lives of others—and how others
might interpret those gifts of time, energy, and even money
that we offer them.

The second basic tool is forgiveness—the ability to for-
give ourselves. We remind you again that oftentimes the urge
to enable comes from a deep love for the patient. Breaking the
habit of enabling is learning a new, healthier way to express
love, but it doesn't mean that the love itself is any less real.
Here is an insight that should help with forgiveness: Every
single relationship is dysfunctional in some way, at some time
or another. No two people can give and take in equal propor-
tions 100 percent of the time. If your wife, for example, has to
have surgery, you are likely going to be spending a disproportionate amount of time cooking the meals, cleaning the house,
and tending to the kids, as well as nursing her while she recov-
ers. And there may be moments in the healthiest relationship
when you feel a bit of resentment for it. The goal is to achieve
a wholesome balance between give and take—and to learn to
give voice to any minor resentments so that they can be cor-
rected before the habit of resentment sets in.

CHAPTER 4

The Story of
an Almost Addict

ONE MORNING, PROMPTLY at 8:15, Elissa walked out of her house, as she always did, through her garage. As the garage door opened, she saw that her preteen son's bike was right in the middle of the driveway, right behind her minivan, exactly where it had been the night before when she had told him to put it away. She was tempted to leave it there and back over it to teach him a lesson about taking care of his property. More realistically, she knew that her options were to wrestle it back into the garage herself or have a showdown about the bike with her son when he strolled out in about five minutes so she could drive him to school. She decided that she had better muster the energy for another showdown or he was never going to learn to put his bike away at night—and then she noticed that her teenage daughter had left her backpack and her sweater on the picnic table in the backyard. It had drizzled during the night; the backpack was waterproof, but the sweater was a sopping mess. Not to mention that, although their neighborhood was not especially vulnerable to crime, the bike, the backpack, and the cell phone likely contained within the backpack could easily have been stolen. These kids, Elissa thought, both needed a lesson about responsibility. She thought through the lecture she was going to deliver to them on the way to school that morning as she unlocked her minivan and climbed inside— and then she saw the plastic cup she had left in the driver's side cup holder when she got home from work the evening before.

There was a puddle of dark tan water at the bottom of the cup, but yesterday after work, it had contained ice and Diet Coke—and vodka.

"That's when it hit me," Elissa told us. "All of the things my friends and my mother had been saying to me were true. I was drinking too much, and I had been drinking too much for about a year—since my divorce. My mother was the one who had nailed it right at the beginning: It was hard being a single mom, and it was easier to cope when I had a glass of wine or a shot of vodka under my belt. I got angry with her when she said things like that, but it just wasn't possible to keep on denying I had a problem with alcohol while I was rushing back into the house to get rid of the evidence before my kids saw it—before my kids caught on that I was stopping at the convenience store for a couple of cocktails on my way home every night...that *I* was the one who needed a lecture about responsibility."

For many adults, there have been occasions in their lives when they have consumed more alcohol than was wise or perhaps used a pain medication longer than it had been needed for the medical issue for which it was prescribed. These occasions did not evolve into an ongoing issue with substance use. Like Elissa, they were able to wake up and smell the coffee and recognize that they needed to make some changes before they caused any irreversible damage. And make no mistake about it: Being the cause of a great deal of damage was where she was headed. In the quantities that Elissa was consuming, alcohol can cause physical diseases such as liver cirrhosis (damage to the cells of the liver); pancreatitis (an inflammation of the pancreas); and various cancers including that of the liver, esophagus, and mouth. It can also cause high blood pressure, as well as play a role in the exacerbation of psychological disorders. Additionally, it can lead to the destruction of the relationships in the drinker's life. In fact, the Centers for Disease Control (CDC) answers the question, How do I know if I have a drinking problem? by focusing squarely on the interpersonal issues: "Drinking is a problem if it causes trouble in your relationships, in school, in social activities, or in how you think and feel."[1] In Elissa's case, the most immediate and grave harm that could have come from her developing habit was an arrest for driving under the influence or even a much worse roadway scenario. Her routine had become to stop by the convenience store near her place of work and consume the alcohol she bought there on her way home each evening. Although Elissa had been adamant that she could still function efficiently after her nightly cocktails, the reduced reaction time, loss of balance and motor skills, and impaired brain function that results in poor judgment—classic symptoms of alcohol abuse associated with even one drink depending on the drinker's tolerance for alcohol—could have proved sufficient to have caused a deadly accident.

Although people like Elissa are often not addicts, they need to recognize that the slippery slope of addiction is a particular danger to them, and Elissa was able to come to that realization. One of the primary reasons for this, in Elissa's case, was the astute insight of her mother and her friends, who risked her anger by continuing to challenge her drinking habits. But they also did something else: They realized *why* Elissa was drinking—that it was a form of self-medication to dull the emotional ache of her divorce, as well as the fear and real material difficulties that she faced subsequently as a single mom. Intuitively responding to the pain of their loved one, the people who surrounded Elissa rallied around her in her time of crisis, and among the most profound service they offered her was to simply listen.

Although at times—Elissa herself would be the first to admit—listening to her repeat and repeat again the story of her divorce and all that had led up to it must have been tedious, having willing ears into which to pour her grief was healing in a variety of ways. First, the mere physical presence of her friends and family helped save her from the sense of aloneness and isolation that can help push a person toward the solace of self-medication. Next, the emotional presence of her friends and family strengthened and deepened her bonds with them, and this helped to dissipate the sense of emotional neglect and abandonment she was feeling at this vulnerable time. But lastly—and quite possibly of most importance—in repeating her story again and again to different people in different ways and at different stages of her loss, she was able to find through repetition a way in which to tell the story so that it made sense to her. She was able to go back to the beginning of it over and over again until she found its starting point, its first dot—the place that first triggered the ache she sought to relieve with alcohol.

Further, when the realization came to her that her actions were putting herself and her children in the way of danger, Elissa was able to lean on her friends and family as she continued on the road back to wellness. Her mother volunteered to come and help Elissa clean out the walk-in closet she had once shared with her ex-husband. They spent an afternoon wiping down shelves, rearranging drawers, and stuffing bags for Goodwill, and by the end of it, Elissa had the sort of easy-access, well-organized wardrobe she had only ever dreamed about. It might seem like a small thing—cleaning out a closet—but it was precisely the sort of productive and immediately satisfying task that can go a long way to positively impact someone who is struggling with a pessimistic state of mind.

Elissa's friends were there for her as well, offering her healthy diversions such as accompanying her on long walks and to regular yoga classes. Diverting the mind from its troubles through pleasant social activities, meditation, and especially exercise can help put those troubles in perspective. And we should never underestimate the therapeutic advantages of sharing laughter with friends; laughter is a powerful antidote to both emotional and physical pain because it actually creates physiological changes in the body. Laughter, like running a couple of miles or swimming laps, is a form of real exercise—indeed, this is why, because we work our abdominal muscles when we laugh, our stomachs can hurt when we've had a really good bout of it. Like exercise, then, it releases physical stress and relaxes the muscles. It increases the efficacy of the immune cells, making us more resistant to disease, and it improves the function of blood vessels and the flow of blood, protecting heart health. It also releases *endorphins*. Endorphins are the body's natural "happy juices"—neurotransmitters that attach themselves to the same receptors in our brains as opiates do; they numb pain and promote a sense of well-being but without the harmful side effects of illegal drugs and even pharmaceuticals.

Although Elissa had begun to step onto the slippery slope of abuse, the manner in which she was supported helped pull her away from the edge. It is, in fact, representative of the way in which humans are hardwired to deal with pain and for which most cultures have traditions and even rituals that allow for the expression and consolation of grief.

So, then, the question becomes this: What distinguishes between the person who is able to recognize and successfully curtail substance abuse before she becomes addicted and the person who succumbs to the lure of addiction? It can't be that every person who successfully avoids addiction is fortunate enough to have as strong a social circle as Elissa had or that they merely spend more time laughing. If we are part of a family whose loved one is in the grip of an addiction, should we lay the blame for the disease at our own feet—because we weren't supportive or caring enough, or because, as we discussed in chapter 3, we might have unwittingly enabled our loved one's destructive behaviors?

Certainly not. As we have also already discussed, we don't deal in blame, and that extends equally to the patient and the patient's family; we focus instead on healing—on addressing and changing unhelpful behaviors. Moreover, there are factors that do predispose a person to become an addict— and there is likely never one factor but a combination of factors involved in fostering the addictive behavior of any one person. Like Elissa, people who become addicted nearly uniformly have emotional issues that predate their substance use and subsequent addiction, and they are without question using their addiction to alcohol, drugs, or other destructive behaviors to self-medicate these emotional issues. But it is the degree of the emotional wound—the pain or *trauma*— that the potential addict has experienced, often coupled with the degree of a preexisting psychological disorder, that can predict whether or not she will lose her footing on that slippery slope. People who are most prone to falling prey to the lure of a continued downward spiral of self-medication are the following:

- trauma survivors
- people with anxiety disorders

- people with bipolar disorders
- people with depression
- children with attachment issues, with anxiety issues, with attention deficit disorder (ADD) and attention deficit/hyperactivity disorder (ADHD), and/or with poor societal and parental modeling for dealing with stress
- people who come from families of addiction

In each of the subsequent chapters of this book, we'll take a closer look at each of these groups, at what distinguishes their predisposition to addiction, and—crucially—at how their healing can begin.

CHAPTER 5

Trauma Survivors

*P*ETE HAD EVERYTHING going for him: a happy marriage to a woman he adored; two healthy young children; a good job that he loved, teaching chemistry at a small community college; and two semesters until he completed work on his master's degree—and one morning while he was out for his daily run, he was hit by a car traveling at high speed.

Pete suffered both blunt trauma, the sort caused by impact with an object, and penetrating trauma, a type of physical injury in which the skin and soft tissue are pierced. He was flown from the crash site by helicopter to a trauma center, a hospital that is equipped to provide comprehensive emergency medical treatment. There, a trauma team—health-care workers who specialize in treating serious injuries—rushed to prepare Pete for trauma surgery. In the operating room, surgeons fought to staunch his internal bleeding, remove air from his pleural cavity to treat a collapsed lung, reset his shattered bones, and stitch up his many lacerations. Nearly six hours later, Pete's condition was stable, and his team of doctors was optimistic about his full recovery—seemingly a very happy ending to a situation anyone would define as a tragedy and everyone would consider a classic case of physical trauma.

Less understood, however—because it is less dramatic and immediate and, frankly, has only recently been taken into account as a genuine medical condition—is the psychological or *emotional trauma* that Pete also suffered. Indeed, through the early years of the twentieth century, psychological trauma was thought to be experienced only by men who had survived full-scale military combat—in fact, the diagnosis of PTSD was developed by studying soldiers who had come home from war and was originally called "shell shock syndrome." In the 1960s and 1970s, thanks in great part to the educational efforts of the women's movement, domestic and sexual abuse were recognized as causes of emotional trauma. Contemporarily, we understand emotional trauma in a wholly different and much broader way than we did just a few decades ago. By definition, a "trauma" is a bodily or mental injury caused by an external agent. In current psychiatric terms, a trauma is defined as "an event outside the expectable realm of human experience that causes a reaction of intense fear, helplessness, or horror."[1]

While one epidemiological study[2] of 5,877 people within the United States found that 50 percent of women and 60 percent of men would experience at least one trauma in their lifetime, we believe that the numbers are unfortunately much higher. Who among us will go through life without encountering an event that was, previously, outside of our normal experience? How many of us can truly hope never to experience fear or helplessness, or even horror, as some tragedy intrudes upon our normal routine? When we speak of the "loss of innocence," what we really mean is that event that causes a child to realize that the world is not as secure and well defined a place as she might have imagined it to be; its realities can be harsh, and she is not perfectly protected from them. By definition, the discovery that the world is not what we thought it to be is a life-altering event.

There are many types of extraordinary life events that can serve this terrible purpose. Let us keep in mind, however, as we delve a bit deeper into the understanding of trauma, that it is a tremendously subjective experience. An event that is harrowing to one person may be taken in stride by another.

A mild example of this might be two teenagers who attend the same showing of a popular B-grade fright movie at a local cinema—one of the teens laughs raucously at the low-budget special effects but mostly forgets about what he saw as soon as he leaves the theater, and the other spends months sleeping with a night-light on.

Responses to the same stimuli can vary because what causes a traumatic reaction is not the traumatic event itself but a person's internal reaction to experiencing it—how the person processes what is happening to him. This internal response depends heavily on three things: the person's history, the coping skills that were modeled to him as a child, and the stability of his emotional environment at the time of the trauma. To illustrate what we mean by "emotional environment," suppose that two different families suffer house fires on the same night. No one in either of the families is harmed, and the pets all make it out safely, too, but both of the houses and all of their contents are destroyed. The stress in this situation is profound, the questions painful. Where will each of the families live in the immediate future? How much of the replacement costs will be covered by their insurance? Can the kids still go to the same school if either family has to move in with their grandparents temporarily? How will the parents survive the stress of living with in-laws? How will they all deal with the grief associated with the loss of their family photo albums and home movies? But among the stress factors facing each of these families in the wake of the fires is also, importantly, the intense strain on the parents' marriages as they struggle to answer these basic questions in a unified and practical manner.

Marital stress and how it is managed is, in fact, primarily what will determine how these families will fare in the future.

What do you suppose will happen if one of the families was, prior to the fire, experiencing marital discord while the other was, although working through an array of not untypical family problems, stable and happy? Which one of the families would you bet would survive the fire intact? "Pre-existing problems that people are able to sort of ignore and work around come to the surface [in the wake of trauma] and have to be dealt with," said Ray Cannata,[3] the pastor at a small Presbyterian church in New Orleans, speaking of the increased hours he has had to devote, post-Katrina, to couples counseling.

Divorce rates almost invariably skyrocket as an aftereffect of trauma, although it's hard to put a finger on how the city of New Orleans has been impacted by post-storm marital dissolution. "Hard statistics on pre- and post-Katrina divorce patterns are complicated by the migration of large groups of people. On the one hand, in the years after the 2005 storm, divorce numbers rose in the Greater New Orleans area, going up in one area by more than ten percent between 2005 and 2006, according to numbers from Jefferson Parish's Civil Judicial District Court. In Orleans Parish itself, however, the numbers of divorces actually slipped slightly, perhaps because of the significant population loss."[4]

Still, there is some consensus about the sort of couples who were able to withstand this particular stress factor. "Divorce lawyers and marriage counselors suggests [sic] that while the storm itself was sudden, post-Katrina divorces mostly happened to those couples whose relationships were already in trouble; in other words, Ozzie and Harriet were spared."[5]

Generally, we can say that psychological or emotional trauma results from exposure to an extreme stress that overpowers a person's ability to cope emotionally. The kind of events that can overwhelm someone's ability to manage can be divided into two categories: single-event (or one-time) traumas and prolonged traumas.

One-time traumas are catastrophic events that tend to happen suddenly, unexpectedly, and, of course, only once. This category includes terrorist attacks, such as occurred in New York City, at the Pentagon, and in a rolling field in Pennsylvania on 9/11. It includes weather events both natural, such as earthquakes and hurricanes, and man-made, such as the disaster of the breeched levees in New Orleans during Katrina. Rapes, robberies, assaults and muggings, the house fires the families in our example experienced, train wrecks, airplane crashes, and car accidents like Pete's all qualify as one-time traumas. Significantly, the loss of a loved one—mother, father, grandparent, spouse, child, best friend—also qualifies as a one-time trauma. These losses are critical, life-changing events for most people, and there are very few of us who get to spend any amount of time on earth without losing someone we love.

Prolonged traumas, on the other hand, are shattering events that are lived through for extended periods of time or are repeated again and again over time. Displaced populations who endure life in refugee camps; combat veterans; soldiers in prison camps; victims of hostage situations; survivors of religious cults; children or spouses who suffer physical, emotional, or sexual abuse—these people can all be said to have suffered prolonged, extended, and/or repeated trauma. Indeed, the experience of prolonged trauma is such a substantial one that there is even a category known as "vicarious trauma," which often afflicts trauma workers as the result of prolonged engagement with trauma victims.

This is not to suggest that certain human beings are by nature weak and unable to cope when normal routines are disrupted by disastrous or even merely distressing events. It is, rather, to underscore that emotional trauma is insidious and that we are fortunate to have a modern understanding of it as a real *physical* ailment that is treatable.

*   *   *

The human brain is divided into three main parts. First, there is the brain stem, or the reptilian brain, which was the first part of the modern human brain to evolve. It controls our most basic physiological functions such as breathing, temperature regulation, digestion and elimination, blood circulation, and balance. The reptilian brain also controls our reflexes and our fight-or-flight response we have to danger. The fight-or-flight response leads to hormonal or biochemical changes that determine not only our emotional response but also our physical sensations—the rapid heartbeat or shortness of breath we might experience in a suddenly or an unexpectedly stressful situation. When we encounter a large angry dog while we're walking along the street, it's our reptilian brain that jerks us into action—causes us to flee behind a closed door or to run up on a neighbor's porch or to cry out for help. The part of our brain that does the thinking for us is too slow to be much help in this circumstance, but we have the very primitive reptilian part of our brain to rely upon to stay constantly alert to danger, and that causes us to react instinctively and move ourselves out of harm's way.

The next part of the brain is the limbic system. This system is located on top of the brain stem and beneath the cortex, more or less at the actual topographical center of our brain, and it encompasses a set of brain structures including the hippocampus, the amygdala (which we'll talk more about shortly), the anterior thalamic nuclei, and the limbic cortex. These structures control our emotions and behaviors, as well as our ability to smell things. It is also our limbic system that determines what memories we will retain—based, it is currently thought, on how large an emotional response events evoke within us—and it is where those memories are then stored.

Finally, there is the cortex, which is the most recently evolved portion of the human brain and, incidentally—because the cortex takes on a gray color in brains that have been preserved—the stuff we are talking about when we use the term *gray matter*. It is in this sheet of outermost brain tissue where such functions as abstract thinking take place. Perceptual awareness, judgment and decision-making capabilities, and the ability to pay attention and focus are all located in the cortex.

Through autopsy, the medical community has long known about these divisions within the brain. But because of the development of brain-scan technology, researchers can today study the living brain—that is, we can know how the brain responds, in real time, to the stimuli that it encounters. In studying these responses, we can comprehend more fully the roles played by each portion of the brain.

Take, for example, the study[6] that Dr. Barbara Ganzel and her colleagues at the Weill Medical College of Cornell University undertook in 2007 to understand the long-lasting effects on the brains of people who have been exposed to a high-intensity trauma. Dr. Ganzel and her team worked with twenty-two healthy adults, all of whom had had some level of exposure to the events of September 11, 2001. Eleven of the study participants had been within a 1.5-mile range of the World Trade Center on that date, and the other eleven, the researcher's control group, had been at least 200 miles away but had subsequently moved to the New York metropolitan area.

For the experiment, the participants viewed photographs of calm faces and of fearful ones while undergoing functional magnetic resonance imaging (fMRI). The study team wanted to measure the activity of the participants' *bilateral amygdala*. The amygdala, as you'll remember, is part of the limbic system and is specifically the structure within that system that gauges emotional intensity and stores emotional memories. What the researchers discovered was that the participants who had been within 1.5 miles of the World Trade Center on 9/11 had significantly higher bilateral amygdala activity when shown photos of fearful faces versus calm faces, in comparison with the participants who had been at least 200 miles from Ground Zero.

What the researchers were able to conclude was that, for people who had been in close proximity to a trauma, their emotional responses were, even years later, still associated with the emotional responses to the traumatic event. The heightened activity of the amygdala that occurs after such intimate exposure to a high-intensity trauma is slow to recover—and this can be the reason that a trauma victim's responses to everyday emotional stimuli can be impacted far into the future.

On a deeper level, in the context of this book, what this experiment and others like it prove is that emotional trauma results in a physical dysregulation of a body function. It is hyperactivity of the amygdala, an imbalance in the body's biochemistry, a misfiring of neurons in the brain—and by bringing the body back into balance, we can regulate the function and restore normality.

So, how do we bring the body back into balance and effect recovery? Before we can talk about recovery, we need to talk in a little more depth about how the imbalances manifest. To do that, let's return to our patient, Pete.

The wounds Pete suffered in his car accident and the obvious physical shock to his body eventually healed. But while he was still in the hospital, Pete began to do things that were distinctly out of character. He began to obsess about the things he could have done differently that might have prevented his accident—if he had only taken a different route on his run that day; or if only it had been his turn to drive the kid's car pool, he would have been out getting his exercise at least a half an hour later and the reckless driver would have arrived at his destination long before Pete ever had the opportunity to cross his path; or if he had just taken up a colleague on his invitation to play tennis later that afternoon, he would have surely decided to skip the run altogether. After he was released from the hospital to finish his recuperation at home, Pete's wife began to notice that he was increasingly preoccupied with the safety of their children—he wouldn't hear of the seven-year-old walking unescorted to a neighbor's house, and the sight of the three-year-old taking the stairs without an adult behind him in case he fell would send Pete into a panic. Once Pete was physically able to go back to work, he found it hard to concentrate. He found his thoughts drifting to the accident while he was supposed to be teaching and often lost his place in the middle of a lesson; he postponed resuming his master's program indefinitely because he had such difficulty remaining focused.

The symptoms of psychiatric trauma that Pete was experiencing as a result of his extraordinary life event are altogether too common: fixation upon how one might have acted differently to change what has happened; a feeling of powerlessness, helplessness, and vulnerability that leads to the experience of extreme insecurity and anxiety or even panic; an inability to concentrate or think clearly and without confusion or disorientation. Other symptoms frequently associated with emotional trauma are hyperarousal, which includes sleeplessness, being easily startled, and the sudden onset of tears; physical manifestations that are traditionally considered wholly medical troubles, such as gastrointestinal problems, headaches, and, for women, complicated and painful menstrual periods; and cognitive issues that can encompass the sudden intrusion of unwanted traumatic memories that might manifest as vivid and intense images, as well as the converse: forgetfulness, disbelief, and complete denial. A whole host of emotions can accompany these symptoms—from a feeling of impotence or helplessness to rage, guilt, and shame.

Pete's emotional recovery was complicated as well because it was coupled with severe physical pain, which his physicians remedied with prescription painkillers. Access to these painkillers put Pete in a very precarious position. For some individuals, a traumatic experience leads to emotional pain that feels intolerable. To relieve this emotional pain, the individual begins to self-medicate. This self-medication, as we've already talked about, can come in the form of alcohol, illegal drugs, gambling, sex, bulimia, or a whole array of other destructive substances or behaviors, including the legal prescription drugs that Pete's doctors so freely offered to him.

Once a patient begins to self-medicate, a vicious cycle has begun that brings the individual into a whole new ball game. This is because the patient now has concurrent and interrelated problems that feed off of and play into each other. It then becomes not a matter of which came first—the trauma that caused the addiction or the addiction itself—but which disorder to treat first to stop the cycle from spinning even more out of control.

Pete had some advantages going into recovery for his emotional trauma. Foremost among them was that his trauma took place at a time in his life when his general emotional environment was stable. He was very happy in a strong marriage when he got hit by that car, his career was flourishing, and his children provided him with an iron will to heal. The landscape in which his recovery could take place was a healthy one. But what of the patient who lacks the sort of edge that Pete enjoyed?

A traumatic event can redefine a person's life, and recovery from the event can lead to regaining healthy functioning or to *decompensation*. In medical terms, decompensation refers to the deterioration of a system or structure that had previously worked just fine. That is, when a system or structure is "compensated," it is able to keep functioning in spite of stress or other deficits such as illness or the aging process. Decompensation is, then, the inability to compensate for deficiencies. This is a term used especially in cases when the heart is unable to maintain an adequate blood flow after prolonged, or *previously compensated*, vascular disease.

In psychiatric terms, decompensation is the deterioration of the mental health of a patient who had previously been able to manage psychological problems. It results in a lessened ability to think clearly and participate productively, or even coherently, in everyday life. For a patient who is trying to walk the path of recovery in an emotional environment that is not stable or healthy, decompensation is almost always a detour she will take.

Take the case of Suzan. Suzan was the daughter of a very powerful and financially influential man. She was an attractive young woman, her natural good looks showcased to their best advantage in the top-of-the-line designer clothing and shoes she wore, and it was clear she had indulged in pampered grooming rituals at the most exclusive spas. Her addictions were also "glamorous"—they revolved around alcohol and whatever was the latest hip designer drug on the scene. She was demanding and entitled when she arrived at Creative Care on an emergency basis—the emergency the result of Suzan's concentrated, conscious efforts to present herself as suicidal in an attempt to get her mother's attention.

This was not a new way for Suzan to behave. She had spent most of her life figuratively holding her breath to get her way, and rather than hold her accountable for her increasingly childish tantrums, her parents had always given in to her demands. She really didn't know any other way to get through life.

Suzan's scheme had worked this time as well—Mom had made the call that got her daughter immediate relief, but almost as immediately as she dialed, she regretted her action. Suzan's mom understood on an intellectual level that her daughter needed care, but she had no emotional interest in being part of that care. Simply put, she had no interest in being a mom. And Suzan was very much aware, on a gut level, of her mother's indifference—and it was unbearably painful to her. Suzan had wanted her mother's interest, attention, and tender loving care, but her mom had responded to the suicide threats by sending her daughter away. Within hours of her arrival, Suzan was curled up in her bed in a fetal position, calling out for her mother, begging her mother to respond to the crisis Suzan herself had created in a different way.

What we needed to know in order to help Suzan toward recovery had little to do with the current emergency that had brought her to us. It had, instead, everything to do with the emotional trauma that had precipitated her need to self-medicate with alcohol and designer drugs. What had gone awry to create this very unhealthy mother-daughter landscape?

The shocking truth is that, of the hundreds of patients we have treated for addiction over the course of more than twenty years, fully 50 percent of the men and 80 percent of the women have been victims of incest. This was Suzan's catastrophe. Through her teens and early twenties, she had been repeatedly molested by her rich and powerful father. And, although Suzan had confronted her mother with this horrifying reality, her mother had continued to act as if the incest was not happening and had never happened. But, of course, it had, and Suzan was not his only victim. Indeed, even as Suzan came to our care, her younger sister was pregnant by their father.

It is a riveting if not harrowing fact that, although Suzan was tormented by the trauma her father had repeatedly inflicted on her, she was in many ways as unwilling as her mother and her sister to hold him accountable for his actions. This sort of unwillingness is not unusual at all in cases in which the perpetrator of the incest is the one who holds the family purse strings—especially when that purse is well filled. Suzan's family was entirely dependent on their wealthy husband and father for financial support; they were accustomed to a certain lifestyle that none of them were prepared to relinquish, and so, as a family, they held to an undefined but distinct party line.

Additionally, in Suzan's case, her father not only supported her, but during previous in-patient periods of her life, he had still insisted upon visiting her in recovery. It is difficult, to say the least, for a patient to recover when the perpetrator of the trauma that induced her illness is still so involved in her life. Any healing Suzan had managed was undermined by her father's continued presence in her life and by the blinders her mother continued to wear about the damage he had done to her. Her trauma was an open wound that was constantly being inflamed.

Pete and Suzan are two patients so far removed from each other in terms of the emotional landscapes they inhabit as to seem to be on different continents. But we tell you their stories not to juxtapose the vast differences but to underscore commonalities. For each of these patients, the path to recovery begins at the same place—the first dot on their emotional map.

In order to help Pete heal his emotional wounds—to regulate the physical systems and structures that had become dysfunctional in the wake of his trauma—we needed to help him integrate the traumatic event into his life; that is, to make it an acceptable memory.

An almost universal reaction to trauma is the feeling that one's life will never be the same, and, indeed, often it is not. Pete will always carry the physical scars of his encounter with the reckless driver, and he will likely always have to carefully manage some residual physical pain. It will always be a plain and simple fact of his life that he earned his master's degree two years later than he had anticipated and that his career path and possibly his earning power got detoured by twenty-four months as well.

But Pete's trauma does not have to determine his future. By helping him fully access the emotions that the trauma evoked within him and by allowing him to talk through the event and those emotions until he could find the source of them and feel them without reservation, they no longer had to dominate his life—or his behaviors. In confronting them, he was able to bring them under control.

Suzan's future does not have to be determined by her trauma, either. But for Suzan, the process of confrontation and control are much more complicated. Accessing the emotions that the repeated incidents of incest evoked in her and allowing herself to really feel them were intolerable. She had been raised to believe that she could bargain for those things that she wanted, even if it meant holding her breath until she got them, so it was ingrained in her to bargain for sobriety, too: If only her mother would show more maternal devotion, then she'd be able to live with the horrors her father had visited on them all. Returning to the first dot on her emotional map and integrating her trauma as a hard but very real memory within what was essentially a war-torn emotional landscape was a daunting task for her—one that decompensation allowed her to avoid.

*   *   *

The road to recovery for both of these patients began at the same place—that first dot—however much longer and more rugged one road was than the other.

CHAPTER 6

❧

People with Anxiety Disorders

W HAT IMAGE OR memory comes to your mind when you think of "anxiety"? Is it poring over your books in college, pulling an all-nighter to cram for the final exam in a course that you couldn't seem to find time for all semester, with the fourth coffee of the night in hand? Is it pacing a hospital hallway while someone you loved was undergoing surgery? Is it your second hour on the phone with a computer technician the day your computer crashed—the same day that big report was due on your boss's desk?

Anxiety is an unpleasant and sometimes debilitating state that has both psychological and physiological repercussions, and we have all experienced it to one degree or another. And that's not always a bad thing. William Lee and his colleagues at the Institute of Psychiatry recently analyzed some fairly old data to come up with a couple of pieces of surprising information.[1] They investigated records of 5,362 people who were born in 1946. These records were compiled mid-century, when the subjects were teenagers. What Lee and his colleagues found is that of those subjects, those who had been described by their teachers at age thirteen as anxious were significantly less likely to die in an accident before they were twenty-five years old than those who were described as nonanxious—0.1 percent as opposed to 0.72 percent. This trend continued as the researchers compared the subjects' progress through life with their teachers' assessments of their anxiety levels at age fifteen and the subjects' own assessments of themselves at age sixteen. According to the researchers, "Our findings show, for the first time in a representative sample of humans, a relatively strong protective effect of trait anxiety."

The downside—and there is one, of course—is that the researchers also found that, after age twenty-five, the more anxious subjects showed a higher mortality rate due to increased illness-related deaths. The researchers concluded, "Our results suggest there are survival benefits of increased trait anxiety in early adult life, but these may be balanced by corresponding survival deficits in later life associated with medical problems."[2]

As with most things in life, whether anxiety is good or bad for you is a matter of balance and degree—and learning to manage that balance is one of life's trickier, yet most valuable, skill sets. That's because anxiety is simply impossible to avoid. To illustrate what we mean by that, let's envision anxiety in one of its most primitive images: a crying infant. Although you likely won't remember crying at such a young age, we can guarantee that you did, and the reason for your tears was that you were hungry or cold or tired or your diaper was wet—something was happening to you that was beyond your ability to cope with or control, and you were stressed about it. Fairly soon, however, your mother or father picked you up and righted what was wrong, offering you food or changing your diaper, all the while soothing you with soft words or maybe a song—"Hush, little baby, don't say a word, Mama's going to buy you a mockingbird...."

With those soft, soothing words, you were restored, recreated, de-stressed—and your baseline response to reacting to and recovering from stress was established. As children, we were taught to reconstitute to homeostasis—that is, to balance ourselves by maintaining our emotions at a more or less constant level—and the paradigm of "learned helplessness" took seed, or not, depending upon the responsiveness of our caregivers. But what happens when that baseline is disturbed? Or when we are unable in our busy, technology-filled lives to effectively recreate and de-stress ourselves? Or when the level of anxiety surpasses *on a sustained basis* what a healthy baseline can cope with?

* * *

We generally describe anxiety by using words that tell how we *feel*—fearful, worried, in dread. This is the emotional component of anxiety, but anxiety is more than an emotion. It is, as we've already said, a physical state as well. Let's go back to the brain for a moment. Studies[3] have shown that activity in the amygdala increases significantly when subjects are exposed to highly aversive stimuli—unpleasant smells, bitter tastes, disturbing pictures and sounds. "Some theorists have suggested that the perceived unpalatability of bitter substances evolved to facilitate the rejection of naturally occurring poisons (almost all of which taste bitter). Thus there may exist quantitative or qualitative differences in brain responses to bitter substances relative to other tastes. Given its role in recognizing and responding to potentially threatening stimuli, the amygdala represents a likely site for such differences to emerge."[4]

The hippocampus may also play a key role in stress response. The hippocampus is a small, sort of sea horse–shaped structure buried within the medial temporal lobe of our brain. It plays important roles in spatial navigation and long-term memory; in Alzheimer's disease, for example, in which the first symptoms are often disorientation and memory loss, the hippocampus is usually the first brain structure to suffer damage. This portion of the brain is also closely related to stress responses and has been shown to actually atrophy in patients suffering from PTSD.[5] Researchers have found that the reason for this atrophy may be due to GABA levels in the brain. GABA is shorthand for gamma-aminobutyric acid, the body's own natural chemical relaxant that induces a sense of peace and increases alertness. When exposed to stress, subjects showed reduced total GABA levels and a dysregulation of inhibitory GABA pathways that have "important implications in stress-related hippocampal degeneration."[6]

In short, anxiety is the brain kicking on our fight-or-flight response to a threat, whether the threat is real or perceived— it's our brain getting our body ready to react to danger, tensing our muscles and dilating our blood vessels and the pupils of our eyes. It's why anxiety is often accompanied by one or more of these symptoms: a pounding heart, shortness of breath, excessive sweating, an upset stomach including nausea or diarrhea, dizziness, headaches, muscle tremors, and restlessness. Your third-grade teacher may have admonished you that you were acting like you had "ants in your pants" in the moments before you had to go on stage during the school play, but it's likely you just had some extra blood flowing through your amygdala and/or a temporary reduction in the flow of the neurotransmitter GABA due to some anxiety about the performance you were about to give.

In addition to emotional and physiological repercussions, there is also a cognitive component to anxiety. Cognition refers to the process of thinking, and anxiety throws off our ability to do that clearly. It makes it difficult to concentrate; we can become preoccupied with our sense of apprehension, fearing the worst and checking over our shoulders for signs of danger. It can interfere with thinking altogether, causing us to "draw a blank." In a heightened state of anxiety, we can even misinterpret our physical reactions to stress as themselves dangerous—we can think that our pounding heart is the onset of a heart attack or that our searing headache is the precursor to a stroke. It is no wonder, then, that when we are in a state of anxiety, we are unable to connect our own dots because the anxious state itself hinders our ability to accurately link emotions and behaviors.

So here we are, feeling dreadful, anticipating something awful happening to us; our palms are sweaty, our heart is beating so fast our chest hurts, we're wondering if the chest pains mean we're about to have a serious medical incident, and we're twitching around in our chair checking to see what ghost or goblin is creeping up behind us. How did we get this way?

Maybe some of us are born with brain structures set for a high propensity for anxiety. We call this an individual's "hum of anxiety," which can vary greatly from person to person. Indeed, mental health care for infants is a growing field, and more and more hospitals are offering the option for concerned parents. If a child demonstrates a lack of interest in visual or auditory stimuli, a lack of interest in interacting with other people, problems bonding with a primary caregiver, listlessness, or if he cries excessively and won't be soothed, the child may be experiencing levels of anxiety that go beyond the bit of wailing he might indulge in while waiting for someone to address a dirty diaper.

It would be a major step forward in psychiatric treatment, sparing untold numbers of people a great deal of pain and distress over the course of their lifetimes, if we could indeed nip anxiety in the bud in this way. But the field is too new for anyone to say with certainty that we can effectively diagnose, let alone treat, a potential anxiety disorder in an infant. However, in terms of understanding infant and childhood anxiety, we should simply and intuitively accept that the significant others in a child's life can help the child experience a lessening of anxiety—and recognize that even an infant does experience stressors to his system that are the precursors to real adult anxiety.

Further, although the recent trend to treat infant mental health issues is a reason to be optimistic for upcoming generations, it does nothing to alleviate the problem of the here and now—to help heal the over 19.1 million adults (ages eighteen to fifty-four)[7] in the United States alone who suffer from a diagnosed anxiety disorder.

Anxiety disorders are by far the most common type of psychological disturbance. In terms of percentages, 19.1 million adults translates into 13.3 percent of the U.S. population— and that translates into about one in every seven people. Think of it this way: One out of every seven people you know spends at least a portion of his or her daily life trying to manage some degree of anxiety that exceeds the damp palms and shortened breath most of us typically feel when our teenager takes the car out alone for the first time or the IRS announces we're due for an audit.

But what, then, are anxiety disorders? What exactly do people experience when normal anxiety levels are kicked up a notch—or several hundred notches? Current psychiatric diagnostic criteria recognize a wide variety of ailments that have in common the same sense of abnormal and pathological fear and anxiousness that are the hallmarks of all the conditions covered by the blanket term *anxiety disorders*. Let's look at each of these disorders in some detail, and let's give some real human dimension to these conditions by drawing some portraits of people who suffer from them—the sort of people you may know or work with on a daily basis.

GENERALIZED ANXIETY DISORDER (GAD)

Evelyn looks healthy and vibrant and much younger than her seventy-six years. She's a retired teacher, but she's not retired from life. She eats well and exercises regularly, walking two miles a couple of times a week with a group of good girlfriends. She volunteers at her local women's shelter and serves as an usher at her church, and she and her husband, with whom she has recently celebrated her fifty-fourth anniversary, spend several evenings a week in the company of their children, grandchildren, and their first great-grandchild. It's a grand life, right? It is, except that Evelyn is plagued with a general sense of worry and apprehension. She can't put her finger on what's bothering her, but her fear is persistent, and she has become preoccupied with seemingly mundane concerns. Are the dishes in the dishwasher clean? Has her husband sent in the renewal registration for their vehicles on time? Is he going to get a speeding ticket if he drives fifty-six miles per hour in a fifty-five-mile-per-hour zone? Evelyn's fears are so relentless that she has been known to balk at getting in the car to go visit her great-grandchild.

GAD is an anxiety disorder that has no specific focus on any one situation or object. It is, as its name suggests, generalized anxiety that is chronic and long lasting, and its most common victims are older adults, like Evelyn. In Evelyn's case, because her fearfulness was beginning to affect how often she could visit family, her husband suggested a trip to their doctor. At her appointment, he wondered if a prescription medicine such as Ativan or Valium might help relieve some of his wife's stress. Fortunately for Evelyn, her doctor suggested that before he write a prescription for a pharmaceutical, she try changing her diet. Foods such as bananas, broccoli, brown rice, lentils, spinach, and walnuts are all high in glutamic acid or glutamate, which are forms of glutamine—which is a precursor to GABA. That is, these foods contain the chemical elements that are necessary to the body in the production of its own antianxiety chemical. L-theanine is also helpful in increasing the body's production of GABA. L-theanine is an amino acid that occurs naturally in green tea, and the doctor suggested substituting a couple of cups of green tea for Evelyn's normal routine of coffee. While modifying one's diet won't work for everyone who suffers from GAD, these basic changes can go a long way toward alleviating and controlling symptoms; they made it possible for Evelyn to get comfortably back in the car and visit her family without the use of prescription medications.

PANIC DISORDER

Shelley was at a restaurant having dinner with a group of friends when she suddenly felt a change in her heartbeat and found herself gasping for air. This was an upsetting turn of events for an otherwise healthy young woman out for a night on the town. She managed to communicate to those around the table that she was inexplicably and intensely dizzy. Her friends reacted quickly, pushing their chairs aside, giving her room to do as they advised, which was to put her head down between her legs. She complied, but the new posture did little to relieve her symptoms, which now included trembling and nausea—and a sense of real terror that was entirely out of proportion to her surroundings, company, and way of life. She readily acquiesced when the alarmed maître d' came over to the table and suggested that he call an ambulance—the physiological symptoms she was experiencing led Shelley to believe that she was about to undergo a life-threatening event.

She wasn't. She was having a panic attack.

Panic attacks generally last about ten minutes, although they can be as short as one minute, or they can last as long as it takes for the victim to receive medical intervention. *Panic disorder* is an anxiety disorder that is diagnosed only when the patient has experienced several severe and recurring panic attacks, as well as behavioral changes that come in the wake of such attacks and last for at least one month. Ironically, the behavioral changes can include fear of the onset of another panic attack, which is defined in the *DSM-IV-TR*—the classic psychiatric diagnostic manual—as an *anticipatory attack*. Panic disorder can be disabling, but happily it is also, with correct intercession, highly treatable.

There is no one single trip wire for the onset of panic disorder. It has been found to run in families, which suggests that it can be inherited, and it has been associated with other disorders such as bipolar disorder and addiction. Tellingly, "about thirty percent of people with panic disorder use alcohol and seventeen percent abuse drugs, such as cocaine and marijuana, in unsuccessful attempts to alleviate the distress caused by their condition."[8] But panic disorder can also be triggered by stressful life events such as major life transitions—making a major financial commitment such as buying one's first home; a death in the family; college graduation; or, as in Shelley's case, an upcoming wedding.

This by no means meant that Shelley wasn't in love with the young man she was set to marry or a sign that the wedding shouldn't take place. Panic is, basically, a symptom of stress. The pressures associated with planning what is, for most of us, a once-in-a-lifetime event, coupled with the life-changing event itself, however willingly or gladly one enters into the change, is frequently enough to send even the happiest bride or groom temporarily over the edge. Antidepressants, which work by altering the neurotransmitters in the brain, and anti-anxiety drugs or benzodiazepines, which are to be avoided as they themselves can cause physical dependence, are sometimes prescribed for the treatment of panic disorder in conjunction with a form of talk therapy. We can use Shelley's case to illustrate the prominent role talk therapy should play in this and other anxiety disorders: Antidepressants might have been the easy answer to Shelley's problem. Indeed, they are among the most prescribed class of drugs in the world, and often a short course of a drug is invaluable in treatment. But some savvy intern at the emergency room where the ambulance delivered Shelley decided to try to connect her panic attack to what might have been causing it—to help her draw a line between the dot of her attack and the dot that lay at the root cause of it. Whether a single panic attack or a full-blown panic disorder is the problem, knowing and facing the source of it is the key to getting well.

PHOBIAS

Ashley was afraid of birds—specifically, dead birds. When she saw one on the sidewalk, her eyes would begin to water and she would begin to salivate and start to heave, her stomach contracting painfully. Her fear was debilitating because when she would be on the highway in her car and would happen to see a bird that hadn't gotten out of the way of a moving vehicle fast enough, the physical reaction to the sight of the carcass would kick in even then. She would be frantic to swerve the car over to the shoulder so that she could get out and throw up along the berm. Her phobia was so all-consuming that, because she'd once discovered a dead bird in her living-room fireplace, she could no longer enter the room—and she kept the door to the room barred, lest another bird fly down her chimney and make its way into another room in the house and die *there*.

A phobia is the intense, irrational fear of some specific thing: elevators, heights, flying, thunder, insects, and even dead birds. And suffering with a specific phobia is extremely common—in fact, phobia is the largest single category of anxiety disorders. Nineteen million people—or 8.7 percent of the U.S. population—are afflicted with some specific phobia, and women are twice as likely to be affected with this condition as men.[9] Depending on the degree of the phobia, it can upend a person's daily life, jeopardizing employment and relationships and the person's sense of self-worth as the sufferer finds him- or herself going to extreme lengths to avoid the situation or object that triggers his or her terrifying fear.

The onset of a phobia is most often very sudden, usually happens in adolescence or young adulthood, and may involve circumstances or things that, previously, didn't cause the victim a second thought—but not always. Here again, with Ashley's case, we can see the value of talk therapy in helping her face the source of her powerful aversion to dead birds. In talking through what she readily admitted had been a life-long problem, Ashley was able to recall a potent memory from the time that she was around five years old: Her beloved cat, Tigger, in its instinctive drive to prove itself a capable hunter, had deposited its night's prey on Ashley's pillow. She awoke in the morning by rolling over on top of the dead robin that Tigger had left there as a token of love. Remembering that robin, understanding that it was the first dot on the long road of this specific revulsion, did not immediately "cure" Ashley of her phobia. But certainly rolling over to find a dead animal on one's pillow is no one's idea of a stellar awakening, and Ashley's fear became knowable. She could put a beginning on it. And trusting now that there was a beginning, she was able to visualize an end.

SEPARATION ANXIETY DISORDER (SEPAD)

Joseph, a single dad, got up one fine September morning to take his five-year-old son, Joey, to his first day of school. Joey, as it happened, did not want to go—at all. He resisted getting out of bed that morning, wouldn't touch his breakfast, and refused to get dressed in his new school clothes. While father and son still had a reasonable chance of being no more than ten minutes late for the start of the first day of kindergarten—although dad had no chance of making it to work on time—Joseph wrestled his crying, screaming, kicking son into his car seat, drove him to school in his underwear, and handed him and a bundle of clothes off to his new teacher. "Here," Joseph said, utterly defeated. "You dress him if you can!"

What Joey was feeling was separation anxiety—an excessive and inappropriate level of stress about being separated from a place (home) and a person (dad). Although it completely surprised Joseph—Joey had never before reacted this way to a new adventure; on the contrary, he had always seemed comfortable in new surroundings and around new friends—separation anxiety is a perfectly normal developmental stage in babies and young children; a little over 4 percent of children[10] exhibit some form of it over the course of their childhoods. It is when the disorder persists into, or develops in, adulthood that it can be classified as a true anxiety disorder. But separation anxiety as an adult disorder is just beginning to be understood, and the understanding is complicated by the fact that the vast majority of adults who present with this disorder can also be classified as meeting the criteria for at least one other disorder. Still, researchers make the case that it is its own stand-alone problem and cite extreme life circumstances—living in a war zone, taking care of an extremely ill child—as its catalyst. "Given the importance of attachment relationships in adulthood, separation anxiety may be more easily elicited in adults than is commonly recognized and might be the norm under certain extreme life circumstances."[11] How prevalent is it? Perhaps as much as 7 percent of the U.S. population may suffer from it to some greater or lesser degree.[12]

SOCIAL ANXIETY DISORDER (SAD, SAND)

Richard's mouth was dry although his shirt was soaked through with sweat. His face and his ears were flushed bright red, his heart was racing, and his hands were shaking. His breath was coming in short spurts, and he was feeling dizzy. Was he facing down a mugger? Deploying for combat duty?

About to propose marriage to the girl of his dreams and worried that she wouldn't say yes?

No. Richard was about to get up to speak to a room of about fifteen people, all of them his neighbors and friends, gathered in a small-town community hall to present a plan to their town supervisors about upgrading a neighborhood playground. He had done his homework and thoroughly—nearly excessively—researched the safety regulations the group would have to abide by as they built, but what were the thoughts running through Richard's mind as he got ready to talk about those regulations? "Everyone will be looking at me." "Why should these people listen to what I have to say?" "I'm just going to bore everyone stiff." "No one will want to talk to me again after this." He had showered—twice—in the hours before the meeting, but now he was sure people were going to notice his soggy shirt and see, or even *smell*, how nervous he was. Richard's best friend gave him a pat on the back to reassure him—he knew how much Richard appreciated reassurance, and he also knew how much this effort to be a part of building this playground for the neighborhood kids was costing his friend.

Richard suffers from social anxiety disorder, and he's not alone. According to the National Institute of Mental Health, approximately fifteen million American adults over the age of eighteen, or nearly 7 percent of the total population, have social anxiety disorder or, as it is also known, social phobia.[13] But other research suggests that up to 12 percent of the general public will experience social anxiety to a clinically significant, diagnosable degree at some point in their lifetimes.[14]

The term *social anxiety disorder* is used to describe a level of anxiety in social situations that is so painful, disproportionate, or all-encompassing that it impacts the person's quality of life. Richard, for example, goes out of his way to avoid going to parties, restaurants, or any place at which he might find people who are not "safe." Initiating a conversation, asking a stranger for directions, and even keeping eye contact with his best friend when they are speaking are arduous tasks for him. He has held the same job for nearly twenty years—not because he loves his work but because once he gets to his cubicle in the morning, he can generally manage most of his communication with coworkers and clients over the phone or via email, and because he finds the very idea of going out on a job interview immobilizing.

There are two types of social phobia: nongeneralized social phobia, in which a person has a fear of one specific social activity (say, speaking in public), and generalized social phobia, which is much more common—the sort that Richard contends with, in which nearly every social exchange is fraught with fear of failure or of being judged by the people with whom one is interacting. But as with other anxiety disorders, it's not easy to pinpoint the factors that cause either type. Ongoing research suggests that there may be a hereditary component—that is, if one of your parents suffers with an anxiety disorder, you, too, are more likely to suffer with one as well. Physiology may contribute as well: Several studies point to, once again, the amygdala; this portion of the brain has been found to be more active in patients who have social anxiety disorder.[15]

In dealing with patients with social phobia, however, one finds that by far the greatest determinant to whether he or she will present with social anxiety disorder is his or her life experiences. People who have been repeatedly put in situations in which they are made to feel like outsiders or have been consistently singled out for negative criticism or harsh judgment can begin to adopt the views of their critics. Perhaps, they think, they really are as stupid or boring, messy or selfish as others keep implying that they are. Over time, with enough negative feedback, it may take only a look from a stranger for the person to automatically believe that the stranger can see right through him, too, to all of the undesirable qualities he has come to believe he possesses. Once again, then, we see that the most critical element in healing is to find the root cause of the hurt. What happened in Richard's life that caused him to think so poorly of himself—to be unable to find comfort in a room filled even with neighbors united around a common community purpose?

Richard manages his social anxiety disorder to some degree—he can hold a job and, with the support and reassurance of his best friend, make it through an evening at the community hall. But in some cases, this disorder is so extreme that it can lead to total social isolation for the patient: no friends, no family, no job—just the constant ache and shame that hold the person back from finding his place in the world he sees swirling around outside. Finding the place where the first hurt occurred and tapping into the pain he felt the first time his playmates teased him because they thought he had a funny walk, or his dad told him he threw a ball like a girl, or a teacher wouldn't call on him to read in class because he stumbled over the words—this is how healing can begin.

OBSESSIVE-COMPULSIVE DISORDER (OCD)

Before he can leave the house every morning to go to work, Keith must go through a very precise routine, beyond that of brushing his teeth, taking a shower, and putting on his work clothes. He starts in the guest room, where his wife keeps an ironing board set up, and he makes sure that the iron is unplugged. Then he goes into each bedroom and checks each lamp and overhead light, fan, alarm, and radio to make sure they're turned off. He inspects the hallway light on his way downstairs where he tours the rooms on the first floor, checking that no lights are shining and no appliance is running. His final stop is the kitchen, where he unplugs all of the appliances on the counter and touches each knob on the stove to make sure it's in the off position. Only then can he comfortably leave the house for the day. When he was a young boy, his family lost their home to a fire, so it's understandable that his sense of security and calm comes, at least in part, in taking what he himself believes are small pains to make sure his own family's home is protected from such an end.

Larry, however, has a much more complicated ritual before he can leave the house in the morning. He must rise, for example, at exactly 6:06 AM; the numbers on his digital clock must add up to twelve in order for him to feel safe throwing back the covers and putting a foot on the floor. If he oversleeps or the alarm doesn't sound in time, he must wait until 6:15, the next time when it is "safe" for him to get started with his day; but these few extra minutes of snoozing can throw off his entire day. He has to rush in order to make sure that he takes his first bite of breakfast at exactly 6:24 and steps into the shower at exactly 6:42, and he has to quickly scrub each part of his body exactly twelve times so that he can be dried and dressed by 6:51. Fed and freshly showered, he can then begin the second part of his morning, which involves touching a series of items—his belt buckle, his digital watch, his wallet, his keys, the newel post at the bottom of his stairs, his doorknob, the kickstand on his bike, and so forth—exactly twelve times before he can leave the house. On the mornings that he doesn't get out of bed until, say, 7:05, the day can really get away from him, making him late for what he calls "library time," when he reads for an hour in the local public library and is scheduled to last from 7:32 to 8:31. And that throws off the hour at which he is scheduled to appear at work, precisely 9:03, making him late or even getting him fired again when he's late too consistently.

Which one of our patients, Keith or Larry, has been diagnosed with OCD? Both of them, albeit to different degrees. What is key to understanding OCD is that the patients, both Keith and Larry, are *absolutely compelled* to adhere to and complete the rituals around which they have organized their lives.

OCD is characterized by intrusive and insistent thoughts that cause severe distress and produce anxiety. "My family's home is going to burn down," in Keith's case, although in most cases, the thoughts are far more disconnected from the person's reality. Some of them can be inappropriate sexual preoccupations that involve people such as family members or religious figures, or outré practices such as sexual relations with animals, which fosters even more anxiety and even self-loathing in the patient, who then worries that he might act on the upsetting thought. Others might have thoughts that revolve around the notion that inanimate objects have sentience, or even souls, and therefore all the rights of living beings. Now, everyone will, at various times, have disturbing thoughts; people with OCD, however, attach true significance to the thoughts that others can understand as unreal and dismiss as passing. It is these thoughts—invasive and unrelenting and seemingly momentous—that form the "obsessive" part of the diagnosis.

Compulsive, then, refers to the repetitive tasks or rituals that the patient performs in order to alleviate the anxiety that his thoughts cultivate. In Keith's case, there is a basis—the loss of his family's home in his youth—upon which he has built his fervent task of checking the electrical appliances in his home. Again, however, in by far the most cases, the rites that patients with OCD perform have no basis in, or relationship to, reality. Such activities as repetitive hand washing, taking the exact same route to work every day, or touching objects in certain intervals of two or three, or twelve as Larry does, are not connected in any meaningful way with those things that the person seeks to prevent by doing them—not acting on a troubling sexual fantasy, say, or foiling the death of a loved one. Still, the patient is utterly driven to perform these rituals. For her, life cannot proceed in anything like an orderly or acceptable fashion unless she rigidly adheres to the task at hand.

The other truly key thing to note about those who suffer with OCD is that they themselves, in almost all cases, clearly recognize that the performance of their repetitive tasks has nothing to do with reality. They fully understand that they are not precluding a tragic event such as a house fire by ritually unplugging kitchen appliances just as clearly as all children know that if they step on a crack in the sidewalk on the way home from school, they really will not break their mother's back. They, too, see their actions as irrational—and yet, they *must* perform them. These rituals serve to temporarily abate their fears and allay their unsettling, intrusive thoughts.

Because it has become a bit of cultural humor to label someone who is working hard, or who is maybe even a bit of a perfectionist, as obsessive-compulsive, let us also take a moment to point out the difference between habits and the compulsive repetition of tasks. A habit is something you do routinely that enhances your life—you have the good habit of going to church on Sunday, another has the good habit of taking a multivitamin in the morning, and most of us have the good habit of brushing our teeth before bedtime. A compulsion, on the other hand, is a routine that interferes with your life. Larry, for example, can't hold on to a job for any length of time because everything he accomplishes in his life must be done in intervals of time when the numbers on a digital clock add up to the number twelve.

What causes a person to develop OCD? Right back to the brain we go. Researchers believe that OCD can be linked to the neurotransmitter serotonin, which is well known to contribute to a feeling of general happiness and well-being. But inquiry into this specific relationship is in its infancy, and it has not yet been determined if a lack of serotonin is a cause of OCD or a result of the disorder.[16] Because the research is so new, no medications have yet been found that will improve the quality of life for a person suffering from OCD—not even medications for temporary prescription-drug therapy to directly address OCD symptoms while the patient and therapist work toward a more holistic resolution.

What we can say for sure is that, of the estimated 2.2 million adult Americans who are affected by OCD,[17] more of them are likely to become substance abusers than any other portion of the population. The reason for this is tied to the compulsive traits of OCD, as well as to the feeling of relief from anxiety that OCD sufferers are self-medicating toward in the first place. As well, most people with OCD will choose "performance enhancing" and highly addictive drugs such as speed or cocaine and even caffeine. As is the case with every disorder we have talked about, or will talk about, in this book, the addition of substance abuse to the already-existing biochemical imbalance in the brain makes treatment that much more difficult—and dual diagnosis and concurrent therapy for each portion of the patient's disease, therefore, that much more critical.

POST-TRAUMATIC STRESS DISORDER (PTSD)

Anne was standing at her kitchen sink one Saturday afternoon washing the lunch dishes. Her husband was in the adjoining family room watching a football game, and her eighteen-year-old son was out in the backyard with some of his friends. The teenagers came into the house through the sliding glass door in the kitchen and paused only briefly to tell Anne that they were going to go to the mall to see a movie, a few of them snatching a cookie or two from a plate on the counter as they passed through the room. Anne didn't see her husband get up from where he was sitting in the family room or reach under the sofa. Later, she would tell the police that, to her knowledge, the lock to the gun cabinet in the corner of the room was always kept on; she didn't even suspect that her husband was so distressed and berated herself: Would she have been able to check the event if she'd known her husband had unlocked it and stowed one of his shotguns under the sofa earlier that morning? Anne said she didn't even know until the shooting was over and her husband had run out of the house that it had been him who was shooting at them all.

Astonishingly, while some of the kids were indeed hit by bullets, no one was wounded seriously or killed when Anne's husband, a Vietnam combat veteran, flashed back to his war years and mistook her and the kids for enemy troops. It is much less surprising that it was a Vietnam-era vet who was suffering from PTSD, the anxiety disorder that has as its hallmark violent flashbacks—intrusive re-experiences of the traumatic event that triggered the disorder. While 7.7 million or 3.5 percent of adult Americans over the age of eighteen suffer from PTSD in any given year, a full 19 percent of Vietnam veterans experienced PTSD after the war.[18]

While PTSD is, by definition, the result of living through a dangerous event such as active combat, it is not a disorder that is confined to combat veterans. Survivors of any traumatic event—physical or sexual abuse, muggings and rapes, natural disasters, accidents, or even nonviolent events such as the death of a loved one, divorce, or a financial crisis—may be susceptible. Furthermore, PTSD isn't picky about who it strikes; anyone can develop the disorder at any age. Anne's husband developed the disease in his early twenties; Drew, who you read about in chapter 3, developed the disorder at the age of eight as a result of his father's sudden death in a car wreck. Unfortunately, in both of these cases, the disorder remained undiagnosed and/or untreated for many years until the patients had endured years of unimaginable suffering, and near tragedy forced each to face his illness.

In terms of the physiology of PTSD, we can again look to the brain—specifically, to a biochemical substance called norepinephrine. Norepinephrine is both a hormone and a neurotransmitter that is released in the body during times of stress and underlies the fight-or-flight response to danger. The repeated or protracted presence of norepinephrine may, over time, cause actual changes in a person's nervous system, especially the limbic system. "The repeated presence of norepinephrine in the limbic system appears to alter the sensitivity of ... nerve fibers such that small amounts of norepinephrine at a later, noncritical time period may produce an emergency mobilization response as intense as the response to the original traumatic event. This sensitization is referred to as *kindling*."[19]

But what are the outward signs that someone is enduring PTSD? Kindling is likely responsible for the most harrowing one: flashbacks, which are events that plunge a person over and over again back into the experience of the original trauma, including the physical reactions to the original danger or threat, such as sweating, panting, and a racing heart. The re-experience can overtake a person at a time when he is fully awake, as happened in the case of Anne's husband, or it can take the form of nightmares.

The person will often also show "avoidance" symptoms. That is, she will try to stay away from places or people, events or objects that she associates with the experience of the original trauma—Anne's husband, for example, categorically refused to take part in any veterans' events or reunions. But avoidance symptoms can also include losing interest in activities that the person had previously experienced as pleasurable, trouble in recalling the details of the original traumatic event, feelings of intense guilt about the event, and a general emotional numbness or distancing, especially from people to whom the patient had been close prior to the trauma. There is, as well, a third category of PTSD symptoms: those of *hyperarousal*, a state of exaggerated psychological and physiological tension and alertness. For PTSD sufferers, these include difficulty sleeping, angry outbursts, frequently feeling tense or "edgy," and being easily startled. But taken together, what are these symptoms *of*? They are symptoms of a sense within the person that, through the experience of the traumatic event, he has lost mastery over his own life.

A person who is suffering with PTSD may take one of four paths to cope with the pain of believing that he is no longer able to influence his destiny. He may overcompensate by becoming super controlling and vigilant about every aspect of his life in an attempt to avoid a second traumatic surprise. Or a person may relinquish any attempt to control anything whatsoever and take refuge in helplessness, believing that because she could not control or prevent the original trauma, it is worthless to even attempt to prevent another. At the other extreme of this path is the person who will continually and purposefully place himself in harm's way in order to "prove" to himself that *this time* he can master the situation—a combat veteran, for instance, who repeatedly gets into fights in civilian life.

The final path is, of course, that of self-medication, addressing the pain with some substance that will immediately relieve it. Over the long term, of course, this strategy leads only to more suffering for the individual and his family as his life is complicated by all of the additional problems that come with addiction. The only true way for the person to relieve the pain and regain the lost sense of control is to uncover the source of his anxiety and to connect with and confront the emotions that it provokes. None of us, after all, can control all the possibilities of life; what we can control is our emotional responses to them and, in this, become confident of our mastery.

* * *

So far, we've focused on the human costs of high anxiety. But for a moment, let's look at anxiety disorders from a slightly different angle: the cost in dollars. According to a study published in the *Journal of Clinical Psychiatry*, "The Economic Burden of Anxiety Disorders in the 1990s,"[20] the annual cost of managing anxiety disorders in the United States was, at the time, approximately $42.3 billion. That figure included $23 billion in nonpsychiatric medical treatment costs, $13.3 billion in psychiatric treatment costs, and $4.1 billion in indirect workplace costs. Of the workplace costs, 88 percent of them were attributable to lost production due to absenteeism by the anxious employees. The researchers concluded that "anxiety disorders impose a substantial cost on society, much of which may be avoidable with more widespread awareness, recognition, and appropriate early intervention."

But this study was published in 1999—well before the national trauma of 9/11. And since that tragedy, there has been a dawning awareness both in and outside the psychiatric community that the base level of anxiety in our society has taken a dramatic upswing.

Every age since, likely, the dawn of time has had its own specific set of cultural fears. In eras in which weather-related phenomena such as floods and hurricanes could not be explained by science, these events could inspire doomsday scenarios, just as more recently, in the years of the Cold War, end-of-time "prophets" could use the very real existence of nuclear warheads to exploit a population's collective fears that some malignant external force loomed to threaten its way of life. But on September 11, 2001, a malignant external force did not just threaten to change a way of life—it hit hard and real and shattered a nation's sense of security. Our collective stress level hit an all-time high, and even a quick read of the daily papers is all we need to confirm that we are still, almost a decade later, dealing with the fallout of that terrible day. We are still angry that it happened and still terrified that it will happen again, and many of us are still reacting to the event with the anger and fear that preclude the sort of clear thinking that might lead to practical and secure resolutions.

But fear and anger are, in their place, appropriate reactions to the tragic events of 9/11. The event alone cannot explain why we are still so shaken and why so many questions raised on that day remain unanswered. To find the explanation, one has to look at the lifestyle in which the fear and anger are sustained.

During the time of the Cold War—during the time of *that* malignant external threat—most Americans got their dose of world news at the same time: once a day on CBS at 6:00 PM by way of the eminently reasonable, if not downright grand-fatherly, voice of Walter Cronkite. But Walter Cronkite has no heir. By this, we do not mean that there are no TV journalists of Cronkite's stature, but that reasonable voices have largely been drowned out as competing news channels vie for ratings—not to mention partisan favor—by highlighting the most sensational and frequently tangential angles of the stories of the day, twenty-four hours a day, *every* day.

Even if we turn off our televisions and take a respite from the news, the constant stimulation does not cease. We are all plugged in with our laptops, iPods, and mobile phones. We are old enough to remember a time in which getting in the car on a Saturday afternoon and driving out to the lake for a family picnic effectively disengaged every member of the family from the world and its cares. In our modern world, while we give a great deal of lip service to valuing family, the scene is often distinctly different: Dad has his laptop in front of him on the picnic table to check the scores or even watch the game he's missing on the television; Mom is on the phone with her boss dealing with what is not, in essence, a work crisis, but, simply because she is accessible by cell phone, it has become one; the kids are lounging in the back of the minivan, one of them plugged into earbuds to listen to music and the other watching the latest Disney movie on the vehicle's DVD player. Today, we are endlessly available to our bosses and coworkers, family and friends; and news feeds, music, movies, and video games are available to endlessly distract us.

On top of the push and pull that technology and information play with our attention, let's add a uniquely American phenomenon: vacation deprivation. "Few other industrialized countries have as little vacation time as America, where there aren't even legal guarantees of vacation time."[21] According to the Bureau of Labor Statistics, U.S. workers take an average of only 10.2 vacation days a year—and this only after they've been on the job for at least three years. In the United Kingdom, by contrast, workers are guaranteed twenty paid vacation days a year and often end up taking up to twenty-five days off per year.[22]

This unfortunate situation can be partially explained by the economic downturn of 2008. Since that time, many workers have been reluctant to take all of their allotted time off, and even when they do, many use a portion of their vacation time to complete work projects or check in via email and cell phone to their offices; they fear that if they aren't relentlessly productive or if they aren't regularly accessible, they may be seen as expendable. But how productive are those overworked workers really? It comes down to a question of how one measures productivity. Long before the economic shift happened in 2008, the Labor Department found that "manu-facturing output per hour actually declined 0.4 percent in the United States in 2001, while countries like Italy, France, and the United Kingdom, whose workers routinely take four to five weeks off a year, saw increases."[23] As a culture, America has long seemed to confuse being successful with being busy. But putting in long hours on the job does not necessarily translate into producing quality work, and overwork may, in fact, even ultimately jeopardize job performance.

Now let's add one final little wrinkle to this nightmarish set of circumstances: Incessantly stimulated, incessantly striving, we are also incessantly beset with the need to maintain the complex tools, fixtures, appliances, and other machinery that come along with living the good life in the modern world. What do we mean by this? Just take a look around your house. If it's anything like ours, you'll find computers, printers, scanners, copiers, a fax machine, and chargers for several different cell phones in the office. In the living room, there's not simply a television but some sort of cable setup for viewing movies, recording TV shows, and listening to music—possibly all in surround sound. In the garage, there are cars that have to have their oil changed and their tires rotated on a regular basis—not to mention that they have their own computers that are packed with codes necessary to keep them safely on the road. Can you even begin to estimate how many hours a month you spend maintaining, upgrading, and servicing all of the technology that keeps you plugged in? Now turn your attention to the kitchen, where there are not just the big standard appliances that must be kept clean and maintained (the refrigerator, stove, dishwasher, microwave) but a water filter that must be changed every three months, knives that must be kept sharpened, and any number of smaller appliances (toaster, coffeemaker, food processor, blender, juicer) that may, at any time, stop working and need to be replaced. Maybe there's a treadmill in the bedroom and possibly a second television. In the laundry room, there is a washer and a dryer, of course. To take care of your backyard, you probably have a mower, an edger, electric hedge clippers, and a power washer, and to enjoy it, you might have a grill, an outdoor sound system, a hot tub, a pool, and lawn furniture with cushions that can't be left out in the rain. We've come a long way from the time when outdoor fun meant that there was a swing set in the backyard, standard homework tools were paper and pencil, and two-car families were the exception. Most of us would be lost these days without a computer and a cell phone; we would be less informed and less able to function efficiently in both our business and social worlds. But there is a cumulative and collective burden in taking care of the things that are supposed to make our lives easier, healthier, and just plain more fun.

And it is not only our personal technology and other appliances that experts tell us are stressing us out. Worries about technology stretch to include general anxiety about the global installation of smart grids to power all of our small appliances and the impact of electronic voting systems on national elections. Health concerns don't stop with clean water filters but extend to the transmission of diseases from HIV to bird flu to mosquitoes that may or may not carry eastern equine encephalitis.

In the post-9/11 era, according to the American Psychological Association, 43 percent of all adults in the United States suffer adverse health effects from stress.[24] More than one-third of Americans say they have had an illness that was primarily caused by stress,[25] two-thirds of office visits to family physicians are due to stress-related symptoms,[26] and fully 64 percent of Americans feel the need to take steps to reduce the stress levels in their lives.[27]

From the frustration of our printers jamming to the fear of global climate change, from the satellite losing reception on the night that our favorite show has its season premier to thinking about the national debt, the cost of war, and mercury-laden seafood, the list of what puts stress on us and causes heightened anxiety goes on and on. Robert D. Stolorow, a clinical professor of psychiatry at the school of medicine at the University of California, Los Angeles, sums it up succinctly:

> I describe our era as an Age of Trauma because the tranquilizing illusions of our everyday world seem in our time to be severely threatened from all sides—by global diminution of natural resources, by global warming, by global nuclear proliferation, by global terrorism, and by global economic collapse. These are forms of collective trauma in that they threaten to obliterate the basic framework with which we as members of our particular society have made sense out of our existence. They create a vague state of anxiety—an existential anxiety, about our own existence and the existence of all those whom we love.[28]

The hum of our collective anxiety vibrates just beneath the surface. It bursts into the open in fits and starts—road rage, workplace and school shootings, political anger—catching even the most serene among us unaware.

In outlining in such detail the types of anxiety disorders and their prevalence—as well as in focusing your attention on the underlying collective, cultural anxiety that is upping the ante for all of us—our intention is to give you some insight into the crushing sense of insecurity and fear that people who suffer from diagnosable disorders experience on a day-to-day basis. It is this unbearable sense of vulnerability and dread that leads many of them to turn to self-medication. They try to loosen the grip of the pain with alcohol or drugs, sex or binge eating, gambling, and even nicotine. Anxiety disorders and substance abuse simply and commonly go hand in hand—indeed, people who are afflicted with them are two to three times more likely to have a substance-abuse problem at some point in their lives than the population at large.[29]

People who are highly anxious will also tend to use prescription medications to lessen their anxiety. Antianxiety drugs, also known as "anxiolytics" and, commonly, as sedatives, work to abate anxiety by depressing the central nervous system (CNS) and slowing brain function. Their use produces an often pleasant, drowsy, calm feeling, and they can lead to the most restful sleep a highly nervous person has possibly ever experienced. Over time, however, tolerance for the drug develops, and larger and larger doses are needed to achieve the same calming effect. For these reasons, antianxiety meds are the most abused class of drugs in the United States, whether they are obtained legally through a prescription or from the thriving "downer" black market. Antianxiety medication is, bluntly, addictive and can quickly become part of an addiction triangle: anxiety + taking medication = dependency.

While there are times when a short course of antianxiety medication is helpful and can be of benefit in treatment, we stress that "short course" is the operative phrase. There are always other, deeper emotional reasons for the state of high anxiety, and those reasons need to be understood and worked through for the anxiety to recede.

Think again of the road we talked about at the very beginning of this book—the emotional map of the patient's life. In treatment, we walk with the patient along this road. Some days we can walk metaphorical miles, some days we can walk only a few steps, and some days are all about the detours. But the goal is to retrace the route until we arrive at the place where the anxiety began. When we locate this place, the patient can make the connection between the painful emotions she is feeling and the behaviors she is exhibiting in response to the pain. *She can know where the anxiety is coming from.*

Say that you are sitting at your desk trying to get a little work done. All of a sudden you feel a quick, intense itch on your foot. Immediately, your hand moves to the spot where you felt the itch in your instinctive attempt to do something to alleviate it. You scratch the spot, feel better, and then go back to work. Soon enough, however, you feel another itch, and then another, and another. You're scratching furiously now, working to abate the terrible sensation, and while you're scratching, you're beginning to realize that you could scratch all day but the irritation is not going to go away. Your next logical move is to figure out *why* you feel the need to scratch. What's causing it? When you look down at the floor, you see your loyal dog lying there by your feet—and when you reach to give her ears a little rub, you distinctly see a flea hopping off her snout. There's your answer. You forgot to apply her flea ointment this month, and now you're paying the price. The good news, of course, is that now you know where the problem is coming from. You can go get the flea ointment right now and fix the problem at its source. You are again in control.

Now, this example of your dog and her fleas might seem to be a bit simplistic to you, especially as we have pointed out that there is rarely, if ever, one direct link between experience and behavior. No one's life narrative is a straight shot; there are often myriad factors that come into play in the formation of any one pattern or habit. But Sir Francis Bacon famously said very long ago, "Knowledge is power."[30] By helping a patient uncover the core reason for his emotional pain and detachment and his need to self-medicate as a result, we help him regain his power—and restore his control.

CHAPTER 7

Bipolar Disorder

MOST OF US have some sort of morning ritual. Some of us get our blood pumping with a brisk morning run. Others feel the day is badly begun unless it involves a leisurely paging through the daily newspaper over a big plate of scrambled eggs. For most adults, the process includes some form of caffeine—a freshly brewed pot of coffee at home or a stop at Starbucks on the way to work.

The reason that these very personal morning customs have evolved for us as individuals is that each of us has different physiological needs that we are fulfilling through our chosen activities. The person who requires a morning run might need or desire the extra shot of the neurotransmitters dopamine, serotonin, or norepinephrine that regular exercise releases in the brain. The scrambled-egg-eater—the person who craves protein in the morning—might, on the other hand, need less serotonin first thing in the morning. The consumption of protein blocks the release of serotonin in the brain, which increases alertness and the brain's ability to concentrate; eating eggs in the morning is one way of sharpening our mental focus. Caffeine, as we all know, is a stimulant, and a good many of us like a cup of coffee or tea first thing in the morning to help get us into gear for the day. But how does caffeine work in the body? Basically, it speeds up the function of the brain by binding to what are known as adenosine receptors. Adenosine is a biochemical that causes drowsiness; caffeine blocks the ability of this chemical to bind with its designated brain receptors, thus causing increased alertness.

Now, it's almost certain that when the egg-eater rises, he doesn't think to himself, "Gee, I better eat my protein and block my serotonin uptake." No coffee-drinker gets out of bed intent on brushing her teeth, washing her face, and binding her adenosine receptors with caffeine. They just do these things because these are the things that make them *feel* good. But why does rigorous exercise make one person feel good while another needs a specific form of nutrition to begin to shake off sleep? Morning rituals are as unique as snowflakes because each human being has a unique biochemistry—a unique balance of cellular components such as proteins, carbohydrates, nucleic acids, and lipids that work together to perform, at a molecular level, all the complex functions necessary to sustaining life. Whether we know it or not, our sunrise runs or favorite breakfasts or first steaming cups of coffee or tea are our way of tinkering with our singular biochemistries in order to give our one-of-a-kind bodies what they most need so we can feel our best. We are adjusting a few of the over one hundred chemical compounds found in the brain that carry messages between our brain cells, or neurons, to increase their efficiency, improve our focus, and perk up our mood. Exercise, certain foods, and caffeine are simply some of the ways we have learned to bring our biochemistry into a practical balance with which we can be comfortable and function competently.

But what happens to a person whose biochemistry is out of balance to begin with? How, for example, does someone whose levels of dopamine, norepinephrine, and serotonin are all over the map cope with that uneven distribution? How does this person function when his level of dopamine, say, is so low in the morning that he is severely depressed, only to rise so high by the late afternoon that he is experiencing mania—a state that can vary from *hypomania*, a short period of elevated mood and energy and goal-oriented behavior, to weeks of dysfunction that include full-blown psychotic behaviors, hallucinations, and suicidal tendencies? What kind of reasonable morning ritual can a person devise for himself when he is at the mercy of a physiological system that bounces between a critical undersupply and oversupply of the chemicals that most people are able to satisfactorily tweak with a pot of coffee or a plate of eggs?

Bipolar disorder is known by many different names: manic depression, manic-depressive disorder, manic-depressive illness, bipolar affective disorder, and bipolar mood disorder. But whatever name medical professionals may use to name the illness, they are all talking about the same medical condition. Bipolar disorder refers to a category of mood disorders and is defined by the experience of one or more episodes of manic behavior—periods of abnormally acute energy— often, but not always, alternating with one or more depressive episodes. These episodes are usually separated by periods of "normal" activity, when patients go without symptoms of either extreme.

Bipolar disorder is, however, an elusive illness. No single medication or any particular dose of any one medication will help every patient. Even with the existence of medicine that can potentially help a patient, there is often up to a ten-year lag[1] in formally diagnosing a case of the illness because the symptoms are often confused with those of other psychiatric disorders, such as depression or schizophrenia. It is a very serious disease, and it can be debilitating, especially if misdiagnosed or missed altogether by a mental health practitioner. It is the sixth leading cause of disability in the world[2] and can result in an over nine-year reduction in the expected life span of those it afflicts.[3] One in five people who suffer with this disorder will commit suicide[4]—and, in fact, 20 percent of *all* individuals who commit suicide are bipolar.

But bipolar disorder is also highly treatable—a surgeon general's report[5] indicates success rates of 40 to 50 percent with drug treatment alone; and the stigma that had often been associated with bipolar disorder has been taken away by the many famous people who have been speaking out about their own struggles with it. Bipolar disorder strikes equally across racial, ethnic, and socioeconomic lines, at each gender, and at every walk of life—actors and politicians and athletes like Jim Carrey and Carrie Fisher; Winston Churchill and Kitty Dukakis; Peter Gregg, the race car driver; Ilie Nastase, the tennis pro; and Muffin Spencer-Devlin, the women's golf champion. And "now some of the most creative minds in the business world—including media mogul Ted Turner, ABC-TV producer Bill Liechtenstein, and department store magnate Robert Campeau—have admitted they have bipolar disorder. Other high-achieving business people—including real estate developers, senior executives, and other members of the corporate and professional elite—also are starting to come forward, leading to a new definition of manic depression as 'CEO's disease.'"[6]

According to the National Institute of Mental Health (NIMH), bipolar disorder affects nearly 5.7 million American adults or about 2.6 percent of the U.S. population eighteen years of age and older.[7] The average age of onset for the disorder is twenty-five, but the illness can also start in early childhood or as late as a person's forties or fifties. Interestingly, more than two-thirds of people who have bipolar disorder have at least one close relative who has also been diagnosed with the disorder or with major unipolar depression, indicating a strong genetic component.

The statistic in which we are most interested, however, in the context of this book is the one associating bipolar disorder with addiction. It is simply one of the most frequent disorders associated with addiction: Recent studies have shown that anywhere from 30 to a full 60 percent of people who struggle with addiction also have a concurrent—or *comorbid*—mental health issue.[8] In medical terms, comorbidity describes a situation in which a patient experiences more than one disease condition at the same time. An older school of thought holds that these conditions, while simultaneous, are independent of one another. It is more accurate to say, particularly in terms of bipolar disorder and an accompanying addiction, that these conditions are caused by, or are intimately related to, each other. Alan I. Leshner, director of the National Institute on Drug Abuse (NIDA), has said that while "mental and addictive disorders are easier to study and treat as unidimensional concepts, in reality they exist together and feed on each other."[9]

It is widely thought that one of the primary reasons for this correlation is the fact that the individual with bipolar disorder is seeking to self-medicate to balance her brain chemistry—to get control of the supply of neurotransmitters circulating in their neural pathways and stabilize them. At its core, as we have already discussed, bipolar disorder is a disorder of altered brain chemistry. For the most part, those with this disorder need to be on medication in order to maintain a stable balance. But the medication must be prescribed and regulated by a doctor, as no one medication or standard dosage of one medication will be a cure-all for every patient. And surely, while attempting to self-stabilize brain chemistry with alcohol, cocaine, or some other substance can be seen as a person's desperate and even understandable attempt at relief, it is a path to certain disaster. In order to understand the intense pain the disorder imposes on those it afflicts, let's look at the disorder in more detail.

Bipolar disorder, as we have said, is distinguished by swings or cycles between two extreme states of behavior—depression and mania. It is a difficult disorder to diagnose, even for professionals, because there is no strict consistency between the frequency or intensity of the cycles of depression and mania nor, indeed, is depression always a clear part of the symptoms a person may experience. Because symptoms vary widely from person to person with no one clear manifestation of a "typical" bipolar profile, in the psychiatric literature, bipolar disorder is conceptualized as a spectrum disorder. This means that the intensity of the affliction and frequency of the episodic cycles that each individual experiences will fall somewhere upon a scale, from mild symptoms to extreme cases. And even within this spectrum or scale, there is not yet any clear consensus as to how many subtypes of bipolar disorder there really are. Three specific subtypes and one nonspecified type currently exist in the *DSM-IV-TR*.[10]

- **Bipolar I Disorder**
  This subtype of the disorder is characterized by manic episodes, whether there has been one or more, and the type of the most recent episode experienced by the person. While a depressive episode often occurs, it is not necessary for diagnosis with this subtype.
- **Bipolar II Disorder**
  Within this subtype, there are no full-blown manic episodes, although hypomanic episodes may be

interspersed with one or more depressive episodes that are categorized as major. This does not mean that a major manic episode cannot occur in the future for someone who has been diagnosed with bipolar II disorder, but it is indeed the absence of extreme mania that makes this disorder difficult to diagnose. Many people who suffer with bipolar II are often misdiagnosed with only depression, as the periods of hypomania they cycle through are often written off by both patient and therapist as times of concentrated and highly successful productivity.

- **Cyclothymia**
  The person cycling through quite low-grade episodes of mania and depression is suffering from a mild form of bipolar disorder. The manic periods may include one or more hypomanic episodes, and the depressive episodes are not severe enough to be characterized as "major" or "crippling." This form of bipolar disorder is often mistaken for a "personality trait"—that is, some quality that can be either positive or negative but that remains a stable, intrinsic part of a person's nature throughout his or her life—although this form of the disorder can also interfere with normal functioning and impact negatively upon a satisfactory work and home life.

- **Bipolar Disorder NOS (not otherwise specified)**
  When a person does not fall more neatly into one of the aforementioned categories—cycling in some more or less predictable way through periods and intensities of mania and depression—the diagnosis

will fall within this catchall category. Again, simply
because the person exhibits behaviors that are hard
to pin down does not mean that the disorder does
not negatively affect his or her quality of life.

Adding to the general difficulty in the clear diagnosis of
bipolar disorder are several other distinguishing facets of the
problem. The first and most onerous is that every one of us
experiences continual changes in our moods from one day to
the next or from one life event to another. Some days we are
in a "good mood," happy and productive. Other days we are
cranky and irritable. Some nights we get a good night's sleep,
and other nights, say, perhaps when we are under pressure at
work or a loved one is sick, our sleep patterns are disrupted
and we can experience insomnia. These portions of time are
not indicative of illness but are a natural part of shifting ener-
gies and/or life events that impact how we view and are able
to function in the world.

Another interesting fact about the disorder that makes it
tough to diagnose is that the person's cognitive functions are
not often impaired. That is, sustaining attention, performing executive functions, and memory are not impaired. In
studies, most people diagnosed with the disorder test as
"average" in these areas, and some even demonstrate superior
abilities.[11] Moreover, the episodes of mania and depression
are most often interspersed with periods of "remission," during which the person experiences no manifestations of the
disorder at all and exhibits a range of behaviors that most of
us would define as perfectly "normal."

The challenge, then, is in defining if behaviors fall or do
not fall on the continuum of a bipolar problem. One criterion
is the frequency of the shifts in energy a person experiences.

To meet the criteria for a diagnosis of bipolar disorder, a person will experience a number of episodes, typically 0.4 to 0.7 per year, with each episode lasting an average of three to six months.[12] But, again, these numbers are averages and not written in stone. *Rapid cycling*, for example, can happen in any of the categories mentioned. Rapid cycling, defined as having more than four episodes or cycles per year, actually occurs in a significant majority of people who are diagnosed with bipolar disorder, and some people can experience ultra-rapid, or even ultra-ultra-rapid, shifts, going from manic to depressive and back to manic in periods of less than twenty-four or forty-eight hours. A true bipolar, in fact, can cycle in a matter of minutes, going from laughing to crying in, quite literally, the blink of an eye.

Further complicating matters is the fact that people can also experience *mixed affective episodes*, wherein the manic and depressive phases of the illness occur at the same time. That is, symptoms of each extreme of the disorder manifest simultaneously. But what are those symptoms exactly?

In general, the symptoms of depression can include feelings of hopelessness, sadness, and anxiety; changes in sleep patterns and/or eating habits; expressions of loneliness or self-loathing, or apathetic or indifferent behavior; loss of interest in activities that were once pleasurable to the individual, including loss of interest in sexual activity; difficulty concentrating and/or dealing with social situations; anger and irritability; fatigue and lethargy; and chronic pain for which no cause can be found. More severe cases can include a preoccupation with suicidal thoughts; suicide attempts; and the onset of psychosis, delusions, and hallucinations.

The "manic" part of bipolar disorder, however, is really its signature feature and the key criterion for how the illness is classified within one of the four mentioned categories. A person who is in the grip of a manic episode has an elevated energy level, and, as a corollary, her need for sleep is greatly reduced. Her thoughts come fast and furious, her attention is easily distracted as if from one shining object to another, and her speech may reflect the racing pace of her thoughts—at a quick clip or as if she is under pressure to form the words as speedily as she thinks of them. During this time, the person's judgment is often impaired; he may go on a spending spree and max out his credit cards, she may decide to stay up all night and paint her kitchen cabinets fuchsia, or he may even engage in risky sexual behaviors, as the sex drive can heighten acutely during the manic period. The person will often become aggressive, highly anxious, or intolerant and irritable to the point of rage with anyone who attempts to intervene with her increasingly atypical behaviors—especially as the person in the throes of a manic episode can feel as if she is on a quest or a mission, unstoppable in a higher purpose—and the possibility of becoming embroiled in abnormal verbal or physical altercations swells. Conversely, the person's delusions will sometimes manifest as euphoria, and his actions will become extravagant and grandiose. This behavior is nearly always accompanied by the person's own awareness that he is out of control. At the more extreme end of bipolar I disorder, the person may break with reality completely and slip into psychosis, experiencing hallucinations and thought disorder, which is a phrase that describes the inability to speak or write clearly because conscious thoughts are disturbed and disconnected and the normal semantic content of words becomes confused.

Witnessing a loved one who has slipped into a psychotic state can itself be a traumatic experience, but let us sound at least one comforting note for those of you who have been involved in such an event: A psychotic event is a scary thing, *but it is also the brain's way of protecting itself.* What do we mean by that? Well, most of us, for example, know where the fuse box is located in our homes. This is because at one time or another, we have all plugged in one too many appliances at the same time and overloaded the electrical capacity. The fuse is the safety valve that trips itself off and shuts down the electric current so that we don't inadvertently start an electrical fire. A psychotic episode is, in many ways, simply the brain's way of shutting itself off so that it can contain the damage that is being inflicted by an overload of unbearable stress. The story of what happened to one of our patients, Rachel, will illustrate well how this natural safety valve functions.

Rachel was in her mid-fifties and an active alcoholic at the time of her psychotic break. She had at one time been married to a very wealthy man, and together they had had three children. Motherhood had been Rachel's prime motivating force all of her life, but her children grew up and left home. The "empty nest" syndrome is itself a major stressor in terms of life events, but in Rachel's case, there was the added stress that none of the children were doing very well for themselves. They were flunking out of college, getting involved in the drug scene, or experiencing enormous or repeated difficulties in their adult relationships. Her children's troubles obsessed Rachel, although she herself was having terrible relationship problems: She and the children's father were in the middle of a protracted and malicious divorce. How malicious? Rachel's husband had thrown her out of the marital home, and Rachel was living in her car. In addition to this already-harrowing scenario was the fact that Rachel's brother had recently passed away—the brother who had molested her for nearly ten years when she was a child, and even after his passing, she could not convince her mother to so much as acknowledge that she had suffered abuse at his hand. She had long buried her grief and anger over the molestation, but now she had begun to have terrifyingly murderous feelings about her mother for having abandoned her to this violence.

One day while Rachel was sitting in her front seat, drunk, a police officer came by to investigate why her car had been parked for so long in an otherwise dark and deserted parking garage, and reality simply became too much for Rachel to handle. She couldn't be made to believe that it was not legal to live in a parked car in the middle of a city parking garage; she became combative and began speaking in an incomprehensible "word salad."

The police officer, naturally, arranged for Rachel to be taken to a hospital where her psychosis could be medically managed. This, of course, was beneficial in that Rachel was at last in a facility where her mental health issues could be diagnosed and addressed. But, in the larger scheme of things, the psychotic break she experienced was also a healthy occurrence in itself. It was Rachel's brain reacting to overload—and tripping itself off before irreparable damage could be inflicted.

*   *   *

People with bipolar disorder find themselves in quite a unique bind: They go through often rapid shifts in feeling states, and while these shifts may be very hard to handle—often terrorizing for them—they are also states that people with this disorder are accustomed to, experientially. Try thinking of it this way: We have all experienced, or have friends who have experienced, the dull dissatisfaction of having to go to a job every day that we dislike extremely. Our boss is a tyrant, the work is mechanistic and mind numbing, or maybe the commute eats up several hours of the day and we resent this additional time apart from our home and families. But whatever the reason, we somehow don't find the time or the energy to look for a new job that would be more personally fulfilling or closer to home. Why? Because no matter how much we dislike the job, we *are used to it*. We know the routine, the intricacies of the office political machine, what is expected of us each day—and certainly we appreciate the regularity of the paycheck that accompanies the job, however much we dislike the work that we have to do to claim it.

Another example, certainly, would be the man or woman who stays in a long-dead marriage simply because he or she can't even begin to imagine what life would be like without his or her spouse. People in this situation have grown used to the atmosphere of the marriage; whether they are abused within its confines or merely bored, it is what they know, and they are loathe to give it up for the not-always-conscious fear that life on their own might be even worse. And in many cases, no doubt, the division of marital assets would indeed make it worse, at least in a financial sense, to some greater or lesser degree for both of them. So they stay put.

The person with bipolar disorder often presents the most dramatic picture: being the life of the party and then crashing into a self-loathing mess. Although this constant cycling is painful for the person and those close to her, it is also painful to give up the all-too-familiar patterns—to give up *what she knows*. This is particularly and poignantly true for older people who are finally diagnosed with bipolar disorder after many years of suffering—they have lived with it for so long that it is, literally, *all* that they know, and they are hard-pressed to see that there may be another way out, another and more healthful way to live.

Let's not give short shrift to this idea. There is an unqualified comfort level for all of us in being simply who we are and doing what we have always done—and being a person who has spectacular shifts in behavior patterns is who the bipolar knows himself to be. This attachment to the familiar may be part of the reason that, although bipolar disorder is highly treatable, full recovery from it is so rare. Only 43 percent of patients—less than half of those diagnosed—are able to achieve a full, functional recovery.[13]

Further, there is a marked tendency in bipolar patients to, with medications and traditional therapy, attain completely asymptomatic behavior patterns only to take themselves off of their prescription medications and devolve right back into the familiar cyclical patterns. Typically, a patient will try to go off her meds several times in the treatment process, at which point the patient often begins, once again, to self-medicate. And when the patient self-medicates, he is not achieving a long-lasting state of balance—he is only adding a chemical dependency to an already-compromised brain chemistry.

What steps can we take in treatment that will help the bipolar patient to avoid relapse into both the disorder and the addiction that all too frequently accompanies the diagnosis? We have found, in our practice, that ninety-nine out of one hundred patients respond well to prescription medications—and we cannot state clearly enough that, for a person whose brain chemistry is organically compromised, these prescription medications can be a godsend. The challenge is, again, finding the right medication for the right patient and working with the patient to find the optimal dose of that medication.

Most often, the primary medication is a mood stabilizer such as lithium carbonate or lamotrigine. Both of these drugs are effective in preventing relapses into mania, and lamotrigine is also effective in preventing depression. Topiramate is also sometimes used as a mood stabilizer, although this use of the drug is what is called "off-label," as it is primarily an anticonvulsant, and extreme care must be taken with the dosage, as it can have significant side effects, such as cognitive impairment.

In patients who experience acute manic episodes, an antipsychotic drug such as chlorpromazine, olanzapine, or quetiapine can be useful, as can antidepressants, although these should be used in conjunction with a mood stabilizer, as antidepressants alone can actually trigger symptoms of the disorder, such as hypomania, in a bipolar patient. They can also act as sedatives, which can blunt the patient's mood and make her feel emotionally numb or as if the medication isn't working. Again, it is only in working closely with the patient that, together, the patient and the therapist can tweak the prescriptions and their dosages to discover the right cocktail to be effective in conjunction with the patient's own unique biochemical needs.

Along with adding a prescription cocktail to the patient's daily schedule, we also recommend that the patient dispense with the drug of caffeine in his morning routine. Caffeine can cause irritability, which can lead to the patient's mood becoming destabilized and/or it can lead to a manic episode.

Sleep is also a major component in bipolar disorder relapse. Along with mood, the patient's sleep pattern must be regulated and become consistent. A patient who is sleeping too little might find that lack of sleep induces a manic state, whereas too much sleep can indicate a return to the depressed state. There is some speculation that a hypersensitivity of the melatonin receptors in the eyes might be an indicator of bipolar disorder—and melatonin, a substance produced in the pineal gland of humans, is part of the physiological system that regulates our sleep-wake cycle. Normalizing a patient's circadian rhythms is a crucial part of maintaining recovery.

In recovery, we also put a great deal of emphasis on developing skills for stress management. As we have stated before, we are all subject to stress in our lives. We all consistently undergo the daily stresses of job or career, homemaking, and maintaining relationships—and many of us have developed healthy ways to mitigate the natural stress that comes with life. We take strenuous walks, enjoy long soaks in tubs of hot water, or schedule an evening out with friends when we feel the need for calm and peace and release. Many of us have learned, as well, how to translate our stress management skills when life ups the ante on us—when we are faced with a major life-changing event such as relocation to a new city or the death of a loved one. Unfortunately, the stress management tool that addicts rely upon is their addiction itself, and in treatment, they need to learn newer, healthier skills to replace these old, destructive habits.

But the biggest mood destabilizer is—you might have already guessed this—the self-medicating addictive behaviors themselves. How do we overcome the patient's often lifetime need to try to tweak her own brain chemistry with nonprescription substances and convince her to stay on the appropriate course of prescription drugs?

At Creative Care, we use the diagnosis of bipolar disorder to prescribe the medications that will help to mitigate the patient's biochemically induced symptoms, but we do not use it as a reference point for behaviors. We help the person with a bipolar disorder understand his medical condition, but we link the behaviors he manifests firmly to the emotional states that motivate his actions. For example, the time period that precedes a manic episode is frequently one of escalating depression and anxiety. What we want to find out is what life event or relationship issue triggered the sadness? What is the context for his anxiety?

These are all too often frightening questions for patients. To know and then be able to predict their individual and frequently idiosyncratic behavior patterns—the moods, thought processes, and/or actions that, for him or her, characteristically precede the onset of a manic or depressive episode—is hard work, and discovering the answers means they will no longer have an emotional crutch to lean on as they stumble into the familiar territory of depression or mania. This is why a therapeutic alliance between the patient and a trusted therapist is so crucial. Patients are going to learn to connect the dots between their feeling states and their actions so that they are able to achieve and maintain a balanced state when confronted with the circumstances that trigger their illness, and they need a competent, reliable guide as they negotiate this new path. But if bipolar people can identify their own specific symptoms in their nascent stages, then they have a measure of control in how they will experience and deal with them. They can take the actions that will prevent the symptoms from blossoming into yet another full-blown episode of depression or mania.

They can lead a normal life—with all of the rewards and benefits and attendant stresses and pressures that "normal life" implies.

CHAPTER 8

❦

Depression and Addiction

*I*T CAN SEEM, these days, as if nearly everyone suffers from depression. We've all seen them—the television spots, magazine ads, and Internet banners that advertise antidepressant drugs. There can seem to be more of them—or at least as many of them—than there are for Sudafed or other cures for the common cold. The television spots often feature otherwise healthy-looking adults walking with hunched shoulders, holding their heads in their hands, or staring at the camera in an anguish of sadness over a background of soft, poignant music while the soothing, authoritative voice of the announcer spells out the benefits of drugs sold under such names as Lexapro, Paxil, Prozac, or Zoloft in relieving depression. The print ads usually feature models wearing the most serene of expressions, implying that their peace of mind was restored after starting a program of the drug in question. The advertisements make it seem pretty clear-cut: Take this drug—your depression will go away, and you, too, will be happy.

But what is depression? That's the topic we're going to go into detail about in this chapter. But first, let's focus on what the pharmaceutical manufacturers of the aforementioned drugs claim that it is: a body's lack of the neurotransmitter serotonin. All of these drugs were developed in response to this theory—that is, they are all selective serotonin re-uptake inhibitors (SSRIs), meaning that they work by increasing the amount of serotonin to a person's brain. This is not altogether an unreasonable theory.

In 1965, a researcher named Joseph Schildkraut hypothesized that depression was linked with the lack of a specific neurotransmitter, namely norepinephrine. Norepinephrine is both a hormone, which is released in the body in times of stress, and a neurotransmitter that exerts influence over a large area of the brain, triggering alertness and arousal. Later researchers zeroed in on serotonin as the more likely neurotransmitter—and they were *likely* right. We have seen for ourselves anecdotal evidence of the relief that such SSRI medications can provide to our patients, so we would be among the last to question the drugs' general benefits. But what is important to note here is that we see these benefits in the context of using the drugs in conjunction with traditional and ongoing therapy, *not from the use of the prescription drugs alone.*

We'll talk more about the importance of using antidepressants only under the supervision of a qualified health-care provider in a few paragraphs. For the moment, let's focus on the efficacy of SSRIs from a scientific point of view. Advertisements for the drugs in question claim, in various ways and to varying degrees, that they will help restore the serotonin "balance" in a person's brain, thus providing a cure for the person's depression. But in the almost fifty years since Schildkraut first put forth his hypothesis, there is still "no scientifically established ideal 'chemical balance' of serotonin."[1] There is a very good reason for this lack—primarily that science has not yet found a way to measure the amount of serotonin in a living brain. If we don't know how much serotonin is supposed to be circulating in a human brain, how can we suppose to know what a typical balance is or if there *is* a typical balance that works for every human being? Remember: Each person's biochemistry is as unique as a snowflake. An amount of serotonin that is right for one person may not be right for you.

As we said, however, we can see from our own observations that SSRI drugs can be a helpful part of a patient's
recovery; often a short course of an antidepressant can serve
to help stabilize the patient's mood so that he is better prepared to work productively through psychotherapy for, and
recovery from, his disorder. Still it is simply incorrect to make
the broad suggestion that a class of drugs can restore the
brain's balance of a neurotransmitter we don't yet even have
the tools to measure. Certainly it is simplistic to put forward
that any drug alone, which acts on only one of at least one
hundred neurotransmitters, can "restore balance" to a system
as complex and still mysterious as the human brain.

So, what we know so far is that science is not yet fully able
to say exactly how antidepressant medication works. What we
do know is that even as these drugs can help a lot of people
in stabilizing and elevating their mood, they also come with a
warning list of side effects that, depending on the degree of a
person's depression, might or might not make the drug seem
so very worthwhile. Let's take a look, as an example, at the side
effects the manufacturers of Lexapro report in their literature:
"In clinical trials, the most common side effects associated with
Lexapro treatment in adults were nausea, insomnia (difficulty
sleeping), ejaculation disorder (primarily ejaculation delay),
fatigue and drowsiness, increased sweating, decreased libido,
and anorgasmia (difficulty achieving orgasm). Side effects
in pediatric patients were generally similar to those seen in
adults; however, the following additional side effects were
commonly reported in pediatric patients: back pain, urinary
tract infection, vomiting, and nasal congestion."[2] But "these
are not all the possible side effects with Lexapro. Please see the
Important Risk Information, including boxed warning at the
bottom of this page, and the **full Prescribing Information**."[3]

While insomnia and an inability to reach orgasm might seem dreadful enough to most people, when you click on the link that takes you to Lexapro's "Important Risk Information," you face these words:

> Antidepressants increased the risk of suicidal think-ing and behavior (suicidality) in children, adolescents, and young adults in short-term studies of depression and other psychiatric disorders. Depression and cer-tain other psychiatric disorders are themselves associ-ated with increases in the risk of suicide. All patients starting antidepressant therapy should be monitored appropriately and observed closely. Families and care-givers should discuss with the healthcare provider right away any observations of worsening depression symptoms, suicidal thinking and behavior, or unusual changes in behavior. Lexapro is not approved for use in patients less than 12 years of age.[4]

These warnings are representative of the standard ones found on all of the drugs we have just been talking about. Plainly put, antidepressants can increase the risk of suicide among their users. Antidepressants have their place; they are a valu-able tool for a therapist treating a patient with a clinical con-dition. But their real usefulness has been overshadowed by the casual, pop culture way in which they are being dis-pensed. As even the drug manufacturers concede, these drugs must be used only under the care of a competent health-care professional—that is, someone who is trained in mental health care.

The problem is, they are not being used in this manner. The number of Americans who are taking antidepressant medications has doubled since 1996. "Yet the majority [of those people] weren't being treated for depression. Half of those taking antidepressants used them for back pain, nerve pain, fatigue, sleep difficulties, or other problems."[5] And here's the worst part: During the same time period, "among users of antidepressants, the percentage receiving psychotherapy fell from 31% to less than 20%.... About 80% of patients were treated by doctors other than psychiatrists."[6]

Let us restate that. Of the approximately twenty-seven million Americans—about 10 percent of the total population—who are currently taking, on a regular basis, a medication that can increase the user's risk of suicide, only 20 percent are concurrently receiving therapy from a doctor who is trained in mental health care. Further, this unsettling trend is true not just for adults but also for children. "At least half of U.S. children who take antidepressants aren't in therapy ... and that delays recovery while greatly increasing the number of kids on the medication who are suicidal."[7]

How did a situation that is this potentially dangerous to people come to be? Part of the reason is direct-to-consumer (DTC) advertising. The United States and New Zealand are the only two countries in the world that permit pharmaceutical companies to market their products directly to the end user. This is a rather new approach to marketing for this industry, as traditionally they had marketed only to physicians who would, of course, be prescribing the medications for their patients. But since 1997, when the U.S. Food and Drug Administration (FDA) issued new, more lenient guidelines[8] for DTC advertising for the pharmaceutical industry, there has been a fivefold increase in DTC advertising budgets, which have gone up from $55 billion in 1991.[9]

As with many situations in life, it isn't crystal clear if DTC advertising is always a good thing or always a bad one. In the plus column, there is really very little room for doubt that an informed consumer is a desirable thing. A patient who is knowledgeable about her medical options is well equipped to work productively with her doctor in managing her own care. But is quality information being provided?

It is also useful to note how the information consumers are receiving is impacting their actions. Only slightly more than half the people who are provided with detailed drug information read it carefully and completely. Clearly there is a disconnect among the intent of the new advertising guidelines, the advertisers' actions, and the consumers' response to them.

In the minus column, there is, as well, the practical and not-insignificant concern that all of the money being spent by pharmaceutical companies to advertise their products is increasing the cost of these prescription medications. But the core concern is more overarching than any we have yet discussed: Do all of the people who are currently taking prescription antidepressants really *need* them?

Let us be more specific. Would these people need the medications if they were receiving appropriate mental health care that included psychotherapeutic support? Taking a pill is much easier, certainly, than doing the hard work of healing, but fatigue and sadness, anxiety and guilt, among the myriad signals of depression, do serve a purpose. They are indicators that something is disordered within not just the world around the person who is experiencing them but also with that person's behavior. One of the common side effects of the antidepressants we have been talking about is the dampening of a person's response to the world. This lessens the discomfort the person feels in his dealings with this world, but in doing so the drugs dull any compelling need to reflect on the root cause of the symptoms. What is the source of the sadness? What event or emotion lies behind the anxiety? Is there a reason for the guilt? In finding the answers to these questions, the individual can learn to adjust his thinking and his behaviors in ways that relieve the negative emotions, as well as physical symptoms, of depression—and, so, relieve the very pain that made the medications necessary in the first place.

That said, depression is a real disorder. At its extreme, it can be enormously debilitating, rendering the sufferer unable to participate in the basic activities of living. This is why the word *depression*, having become part of the popular vernacular, has in some cases lost its clinical usefulness. While it remains important as a descriptor for those looking to convey how they feel in a general sense, we have to look at one other factor that concerns us about its now-common use: Almost 70 percent of all the antidepressants that are sold in the world are sold in the United States.[10] We are forced to wonder if this phenomenon of sadness that seems to be sweeping America has anything to do with the fact that, as we've noted, the United States is one of only two countries in the world that allow DTC advertising of this class of drugs. How much of this epidemic of sadness is true clinical depression, and how much of it is due to the fact that Americans are continually being "pitched" a mental health disorder? Sadness and sorrow are normal parts of life. Every one of us will have greater or lesser reasons to experience these emotions over the course of our lifetimes. But while dire life circumstances—the loss of a job, the death of a loved one, or any other major life transition—can indeed prompt the onset of clinical depression, even these do not automatically do so.

We live in a culture that promotes instant gratification. Are we now faced with the temptation to medicate emotions that are an unpleasant but essential part of the human condition—and so immediately dispense with a fundamental part of our humanity?

Further—although this may surprise you—depression does not in every case originate in a person's emotional landscape. As we do for every patient who comes to Creative Care, we begin treatment by taking a thorough history and arranging for a thorough physical examination. In a case in which we suspect the patient is suffering with depression, a physical is of the utmost importance, as there are certain physiological conditions that can masquerade as depression. With the examination, we look to rule out physical causes for depression.

For example, hypothyroidism, when the body produces too little of the thyroid hormone, can cause many of the same symptoms as depression. Hypothyroidism is, actually, a relatively easy physical problem to overlook, as it's not easily diagnosed. We recommend one of two specific tests to screen for this condition—the thyrotropin-releasing hormone (TRH) stimulation test or another test that measures antithyroid antibodies. If we discover hypothyroidism in the course of the physical exam, we recommend that the patient begin a course of medication to address the medical condition and so allow him to reconnect with his more organic baseline emotional state.

As well, some medications themselves can also increase the risk of depression—beta-blockers or reserpine used to treat high blood pressure, for instance. A thorough physical examination can help to establish that there is no physiologic cause for the emotional disorder.

Even so, the fact remains that nearly 30 percent of patients with substance-abuse issues will also suffer from some degree of depression.[11] So once the physical causes have been ruled out or addressed, then it is time to look into the emotional life and issues of the person suffering from depression. We can't say this often enough: It is rarely something as simplistic as a lack of will power that keeps a person from kicking an addiction; it is the underlying psychological issues, like depression, that must be addressed for the addict to have an opportunity for success.

A plethora of books, research, and theories exist on the origin and treatment of depression. For example, some practitioners employ what is known as cognitive behavioral therapy (CBT) when treating patients who are diagnosed with depression. The theory behind this therapy is that depression originates in the patient's tendency to think negative thoughts or have a negative outlook about the world, the future, and herself. She sees herself at fault for every problem she encounters, and she has no expectation that the problem won't be permanent. In other words, the patient is a raging pessimist, and the therapy revolves around restructuring the way the patient thinks, helping her find more positive ways to interpret events, and then acting in accordance with a new, more positive worldview.

Behavioral activation (BA) is another therapy that is widely practiced. BA practitioners believe that depression is based on a patient's own actions, and even hidden desire, to maintain the depression. BA treatment involves exploring with the patient the ways that she could change her behavior to affect different outcomes and creating a plan to do so.

But Dr. K. remembers that in one of his very first professional courses, a professor explained to the class that "depression is internalized anger." All other things being equal, we have found this to be quite true in our practice. Let us explain how unresolved anger can be turned inward toward the self by telling you the story of how it happened in one representative case.

Jo grew up in an upper-middle-class home in a small town in the southeast. Her family had been prominent in the town for generations—indeed, the family surname was carved in the stone on one of the buildings at the local college campus, and they had donated land to create a local park that also bore their name. Her parents were business people; her dad owned a successful insurance agency, and her mom was the office manager. The family belonged to the local country club, sent their children to the town's private school, and generally participated in all the "right" activities, including supporting prestigious local charities and political candidates. On paper, the family led a charmed storybook life.

The reality that Jo lived with every day behind closed doors was, however, quite a contrast. Her mom and dad drank heavily each evening at dinner and, as the evening progressed, would become belligerent with each other. Their fights, unfortunately, would frequently devolve into physical skirmishes. Jo recalled one evening from her preteen years when her dad cleared the dinner table with a swipe of his arm, sending plates, glasses, and the roast chicken flying across the dining room. Then he picked up her mom and sent her flying across the dining room, too.

Jo wasn't able to recall what, specifically, had provoked her parents' fight that evening, but she had a clear memory of the aftermath: huddling, crying in a corner of the room,

shouting out her promise that if her parents would just stop
hurting each other she would be good. She would get better
grades and never miss her curfew again, and she would start
helping more around the house. Although it had not been Jo's
actions that had precipitated her parents' clash—her father's
anger had not started off at her—she took responsibility for
it. If she could just be a better daughter, she believed, then
her parents would have no more reason to be angry with
each other.

Sadly, as hard as Jo tried during her teenage years, she
was, of course, unable to affect the change in her parents'
behavior that she so desperately wanted. Nothing she did
was good enough to appease her parents. For many years,
she gave them little reason to be other than supremely proud
of her, and yet their fights continued to escalate. The way
that Jo came to understand the situation was that it was *she*
who was a failure—she was the bad person, hopeless, worthless, and undeserving. The anger she should rightly have
felt at her parents for having to bear witness to their nightly
brawls became anger at herself for being powerless to create
peace between them.

As an adult, Jo herself became an alcoholic and a drug user.
She self-medicated primarily with Jack Daniels, marijuana,
and prescription codeine tablets she claimed she needed
for debilitating headaches. She dropped out of college, opt-
ing instead to spend her twenties and thirties in a series of
menial jobs, moving from relationship to relationship, and
just as often from state to state, rarely visiting her parents
and sometimes even neglecting to provide them with a current address. In her forties, she spent time in jail after her
third arrest for driving under the influence and was unable
to attend her father's funeral because the judge declined to

release her from prison to make the trip. That was when Jo hit her bottom and at last sought help.

Had Jo's anger been differently directed, might her life have taken a much dissimilar course? That's a question for which there is no absolute answer, of course. But let us contrast Jo's story with that of a woman we happen to know who shared her own experience with us. She grew up in a home very similar to Jo's—her alcoholic parents fought constantly and often involved her in their battles. Her father, in fact, directed his anger squarely at her on many occasions and physically abused her from the time she was seven until she was fifteen—and then the abuse stopped abruptly. Why? Because one night, while she was at the kitchen table doing her homework and her father, drunk and ready to pick a fight, entered the kitchen, shouting contemptuously at her and scattering her math work sheets, the woman did an incredible thing. She stood up and moved to put the table between herself and her father and then she pointed a finger at him and shouted back, "No! No more! You are never going to hit me ever again!" The language she used as she told her story was much more colorful, but she followed up her declaration by fleeing the house and running to the only place she could think of to find safety—the local hospital—where she told her story to an emergency-room doctor, and a social worker was enlisted to help remove her from her parents' home.

We tell this story not to make a judgment but to point out a fact that some of you might find startling: Anger is not always a bad thing. Anger has gotten a bum rap, but the fact is that when it is expressed appropriately, it can be a useful emotion and lead to effective problem solving. "The concept of constructive anger is . . . gaining empirical support from a recently validated measure developed by Mount Sinai

Medical Center psychologist Karina Davidson, PhD, and colleagues. Described in the January 2000 issue of *Health Psychology* (Vol. 19, No. 1), the instrument explores factors like people's propensity to calmly discuss their angry feelings and to work toward solutions. Indeed, use of the scale with male heart patients high in hostility suggests that constructive anger may have health benefits as well."[12]

We are addressing here anger as distinct from aggression. Anger is followed by aggression, in fact, in only about 10 percent of situations.[13] What we are talking about is the benefit of honestly expressing an emotion in a situation where that emotion is appropriate. It's through the expression of emotion that we create the feedback loop that allows us to interact productively and pleasurably with other people. If you are pleased that your teenage son has remembered to mow the lawn when he got home from school as you told him to do, expressing your approval is a way of rewarding his behavior—and reinforcing his desire to win your approval again the next time the grass needs to be groomed. If you're annoyed with him for leaving his dirty laundry on the bathroom floor instead of putting it in the hamper where it belongs, expressing your irritation is a way to get him to really "hear you"—to take to heart what this small step to keep the house tidy means to you instead of dismissing it as "nagging." Anger, in its turn, can be a signal that you mean business—and by expressing it calmly, it can help deepen relationships by taking them to a new level of understanding. Unexpressed, however, it can become confused and misdirected—and the consequences can become tragic. There are twenty-five years of Jo's life of which she has either little memory or the memories are so troubling that she can barely stand to bring them to mind; in her mid-forties, Jo is finally

getting angry and learning how to express that valuable emotion appropriately—and we are encouraging her.

It is also important to understand that there are many different types of depression. Let us break them down into two
distinct categories: phase-specific depression and incident-
specific depression.

Phase-specific depression refers to states of depression
that last for varying lengths of time, the onset of which is
not defined by a specific, concurrent triggering event. The
incident-specific sort, as its name suggests, is the onset of
depression caused by a describable life incident. While both
of these types of depression can vary in terms of both intensity and duration, the incident-specific variety usually takes
place within a shorter and more predictable time frame.
Unsurprisingly, the symptoms for each sort of depression are
quite similar, so helping patients clarify the circumstances
surrounding their unique emotional state is one of the initial
steps for effective treatment.

There are three subcategories of phase-specific depression.
The first is major depressive disorder, which is also called clinical depression or simply major depression. Major depressive
disorder is diagnosed when a patient presents with at least
four or more of the following symptoms that last nearly all
day long, nearly every day, for at least two weeks: sleep problems (either difficulty sleeping or an increase in sleep time);
loss of energy or feelings of fatigue; significant decrease in
appetite and/or weight loss or, conversely, significant increase
in appetite and/or weight gain; low self-esteem and negative
thoughts about oneself, including feelings of worthlessness or
excessive or unfounded guilt; a pervading sense of hopelessness or despair; difficulty with cognitive functions such as
concentrating or making decisions; and thinking repeatedly

about suicide or death, attempting suicide, or making a plan to attempt suicide. Additionally, the observations of others can help in making a diagnosis of major depressive disorder, as the patient may also demonstrate changes in movements, either speeding up motions or slowing them down, and may not be aware of the changes herself.

We also note that depression may be accompanied by real physical pain that may or may not be a signal that the disorder is present. Depressed patients frequently suffer from headaches, and if a patient has a history of migraines, they are likely to worsen during episodes of depression. Depression also exacerbates chronic pain, such as back pain, joint pain, and muscle aches, and can bring on chest pains of the sort typically associated with cardiac events.

The second subcategory of phase-specific depression is dysthymic disorder. Dysthymic disorder is diagnosed when a patient has experienced a depressed mood for at least two years and shows, as well, at least two of the aforementioned symptoms.

Finally, there is manic depression, which can be part of bipolar disorder, as discussed in the previous chapter, in which symptoms such as inflated self-esteem, engagement in potentially risky behavior in the service of pleasure (such as overspending or having unprotected sex), or hallucinations can be severe enough to necessitate hospitalization in order to prevent the patient from coming to harm or harming others.

* * *

Incident-specific depression may be an easier illness to understand on the surface because the source of the depression is rooted in a definable event or circumstance, and it has been well established that within the stages of grief, depression is an anticipated response.

In 1969, in her book *On Death and Dying*, Elisabeth Kübler-Ross codified the five stages of grief—denial, anger, bargaining, depression, and acceptance. Her original intent was to describe how these stages applied to those suffering from a terminal illness, but she later applied them to the experience of other catastrophic life events, including the death of a loved one, divorce, the loss of a job, chronic illness, the experience of a natural disaster, a diagnosis of infertility, and drug and alcohol addiction.

Indeed, the depression experienced in conjunction with certain life events is so common that there are specific disorders named for them—for example, postpartum depression, which is a depressive episode that some women experience after having a baby. The depressive episode can be a major one, with the onset of symptoms usually occurring around four weeks after giving birth, although the duration can be unpredictable. Seasonal affective disorder (SAD), on the other hand, is quite predictable. It is characterized by bouts of major depression that recur annually in the fall and winter.

There are also stages in life that are known to harbor the potential for depression—for example, the "empty-nest syndrome," which refers to the stage in life for parents when all their children have left home. Even events that are customarily considered happy or celebratory occasions—such as weddings, job promotions, or college graduations—can bring on depression as they are associated with significant life changes and, so, are highly stressful.

What all of the various types of depressions have in common is pain, psychological and/or physical. And when we are in pain, our first instinctual response is to try to alleviate it. If a depressive disorder is undiagnosed and untreated, the person who is suffering with the pain may attempt to ease it with some form of self-medication—and the pain can lead to a greater vulnerability for addiction.

Many people have come to us stating that they began to use drugs and alcohol to deal with the pain of their depression. Unfortunately, using drugs and alcohol to deal with their depression led to an addiction problem on top of the problem with depression. When individuals like these come to us, our task becomes that of unearthing the origins of their depression and helping them connect the dots from the feeling state of depression to the co-occurring problem of addiction. In this process of connecting the dots, we look to bring forth feeling states that precipitated the depression. As an example, many people react to traumatic events by shutting down and refusing to talk with those around them or express in any way the emotions that the event has provoked. But when people shut down after a traumatic event, they begin to internalize all of the negative emotions they are feeling: fear, helplessness, rage, loss. When the individual with a dual diagnosis of depression and addiction comes to treatment, our job is to free the individual from being locked in by his emotional state—to help the individual connect the dots from the event to internalized feelings and his behavioral response to self-medicate.

As we do with patients who suffer from anxiety disorders, in cases of depression, we again sometimes begin treatment with a short course of antidepressant medication along with talk therapy. The key phrases in that last sentence are "short course" and "along with." The purpose of using the medication is not to artificially induce an elevated mood that can be sustained only with the use of pharmaceuticals; the purpose of using the medications at all is to help stabilize the patient's emotional state so that she can be more productive as she progresses through talk therapy.

One of the most productive things that people can do following a traumatic event is to continually retell the story of what has happened to them. In retelling their story, they receive a multitude of benefits—they are able to feel the effect of the events and receive reassurance that they have made it through, they are able to experience and feed off of the reaction of others who hear the story, and they are able to purge the negative emotions in the process of telling their story.

And ultimately, what their storytelling allows them to do is to reconnect with the point where their story began—to recognize and confront the source of their pain. Once this connection occurs—once they have experienced that "aha moment"—they are able to access attitudes and behaviors that will enable them to move through life's events in a healthier, more constructive way.

CHAPTER 9

Children on the Slippery Slope

ALEX WAS SEVENTEEN when he began his freshman year at the state university—a little young, but very smart, so his proud parents believed. He planned on declaring a major in robotics—the science of engineering robots—and was especially interested in the software development aspect of the career path. He had been in a relatively long-term romantic relationship—eight months in length—and although his girlfriend was attending a nearby school, it was a bit of a challenge for Alex to adjust to the separation. When his girlfriend proved to be more adaptable, reporting to him all the fun she was having attending parties and really getting into the spirit of life on her campus, Alex decided he needed to have more fun on his own, too. In order to find a group of new friends to have fun with, Alex decided to pledge a fraternity.

Alex's time as a pledge began comfortably enough. Although the state he lived in was one of the forty-four that have now enacted antihazing legislation, he didn't really mind running personal errands for the senior boys who were going to be his brothers—washing their cars or doing their laundry. And he actually sort of liked wearing the ridiculous hats they made him put on in the mornings; to Alex, the cap with the monkey ears was less of a symbol of ridicule than one that showed he belonged to an established campus group. Although he thought being woken up at 2:00 AM and forced to take a cold shower definitely bordered on the absurd, he didn't want to come across as a poor sport, so he also thought he could tolerate even that. It was the evening that he was corralled in the fraternity's game room with others of his pledge class and told that he would be answering questions posed by the upperclassmen—and would be expected to chug a full mug of beer every time he got the answer wrong—that Alex proved he was as smart as his parents believed he was and drew the line. Since 1970, there has been at least one death on a campus somewhere in America due to a practice called hazing[1]—and 82 percent of deaths from hazing involve alcohol.[2] How did Alex get smart enough to opt out of a ritual that might have proved fatal for him as it has for so many other young people?

The use of alcohol by people in their late childhoods or early teens isn't exactly an uncommon phenomenon. Over 50 percent of eighth graders, whose average age was fourteen, reported in one survey that they had already used alcohol, and half of these children say that they had already experienced one episode of being "drunk."[3] According to the American Academy of Pediatrics (AAP), 90 percent of teenagers in another survey of sixteen- to nineteen-year-olds recalled having had their first drink by the time they were eleven years old. Also according to the AAP, the average teen spends about 5.5 days every month engaged in an activity in which drinking is involved, and 16 percent of those teens reported having experienced blackout spells due to heavy drinking.[4] But if you think those statistics are shocking, wait. It gets worse. Every day in America, more than 13,000 children and teenagers take their first drink of alcohol, according to a study conducted by the National Center on Addiction and Substance Abuse.[5] According to this same study, almost 26 percent of underage drinkers abuse alcohol and are dependent on it.[6] Each and every year, over 150,000 college students like Alex develop an alcohol-related health problem—and 1,400 American college students between the ages of eighteen and twenty-four die from alcohol-related injuries and accidents, including motor vehicle accidents.[7]

Again we ask the crucial question to which every parent is dying to know the answer: What made Alex different? What helped save him from becoming a statistic?

There is, of course, no one easy answer to that question, but in this chapter, we are going to help parents understand the factors that can contribute to their child's ability to resist the heady temptations all around him to take a drink of alcohol and to become one of the "cool kids" who abuse it and instead lead a healthier, more pleasurable childhood, adolescence, and young adulthood.

It has been said before, almost to the point of becoming a cliché, that communication is one of the most important factors in raising a healthy, well-adjusted child. Well, sometimes clichés become clichés because of a real truth that lies at the heart of them. Open and honest lines of communication are likely the most valuable assets in any parent–child relationship. For example, Alex felt completely comfortable telling his parents about his initial inability to adjust to college life and his interest in pledging a fraternity to combat feeling out of place and his sense of homesickness. His mom and dad, in turn, were savvy enough not to accept this information at face value. They were sympathetic to, and supportive of, his feelings—his sense of not quite belonging. They went out of their way to make sure he had a ride home on the weekends and enough minutes on his calling card to talk at length with his girlfriend when he and she needed to do that. They also did a little research, and what they found alarmed them.

His mom and dad weren't alarmed about Greek life in particular—many fraternities and sororities can be places where values such as responsibility and loyalty are honed;

Alex's dad had belonged to a frat and, having had to work
through his college years on the physical maintenance of the
house as well as on making sure he did his part to pay off its
mortgage, had always maintained that the experience helped
prepare him to be a knowledgeable and accountable home-
owner as an adult.

What concerned them were the harrowing statistics
they came upon concerning childhood and teenage abuse
of alcohol and the accompanying projections about how
that abuse could negatively impact the sort of future a child
could expect to live. They'd been prepared to accept a bit
of "harmless" beer drinking as part of Alex's college experience, but the results of drinking at such an early age could
also include increased rates of psychiatric disorders later in
life, lowered success in school and extracurricular activities,
increased criminal behavior, and lowered overall satisfaction and productivity in life.[8] Additionally, as children with
a history of abusing alcohol at a young age enter their young
adulthoods, they are more likely to have to deal with not only
increased rates of psychiatric problems but also increased
physical health risks related to substance abuse, less stability of employment and committed relationships, and, again,
increased criminal behavior.[9]

Suddenly a bit of beer drinking didn't appear so harmless. What, after all, would they define as "a bit?" And would
their son have the same definition? Was he old enough and
mature enough to handle the effects of alcohol, or would he
be unable to help it if "a bit" of beer compelled him to some
dangerous extreme?

This last concern wasn't an idle one. And thinking it wasn't
an affront to either Alex's history of general good behavior
or his mom and dad's parenting skills. It had everything to

do with a very specific physiologic stage of normal human growth—specifically, the growth and development of the brain. At seventeen, Alex's age, a young person's brain is not yet quite complete.

As scientific research has progressed, we have been able, through the development of technologies such as magnetic resonance imaging (MRI), to learn more and more about the living brain. What we now know for sure about the adolescent brain is that the limbic system and amygdala regions of it—the regions of the brain associated with aggression and impulse—are highly active and, so, exert a great deal of influence over a teenager's behavior. But the frontal lobe of the brain—primarily the area known as the prefrontal cortex, which is the center of such advanced brain functions as abstract thinking, planning and judgment, recognition of consequences, and impulse control—is not fully developed in humans until they are in their early twenties.[10]

Does this mean that we can't trust young adults with any decision, at least not until they're twenty-two or so, when scientists tell us that their gray matter is fully formed? Certainly not. Many young adults, like Alex, demonstrate impressive decision-making skills, particularly in focused situations. Often referred to as "cold cognition," a focused decision-making scenario is one in which only the facts of a situation come into play in the decision-making process. In a test-taking situation, as a simple example, even the youngest children, when confronted with a multiple-choice test, should be able to test the facts they know against the answers that are presented to them and choose the correct answer.

"Hot cognition," on the other hand, is decision-making that is influenced by all of the desires and emotions surrounding the given situation. To illustrate, let's look at a child who has to choose between work and play: If he goes to the ball game after school, he won't have time to study for that big test tomorrow. The child may know that he has to schedule the time to study, but if his friends are headed to the ballpark, it could be hard for the child not to tag along, too. His brain isn't yet able to incorporate long-term planning or the delay of gratification into his thinking process.

But good adult judgment includes characteristics such as long-term thinking and is influenced by not only cognitive thinking but also psychosocial factors. "Psychosocial factors" refer to one's ability to be aware of the environment around oneself and to interact with it pleasurably and productively. An example of this would be the child thinking that if he doesn't make the time to study, he is going to get a bad grade and disappoint his parents, his teacher, and himself—and realizing that he may not even be able to graduate with his class if he keeps getting bad grades.

What this boils down to is simple: In emotionally charged situations, such as being pressured by peers to head off to the ballpark instead of the school library to study—or to, as in Alex's case, have a drink—teenage and young-adult behaviors are more likely to be influenced by the areas of the brain that control and regulate emotion rather than reason.[11] Play ball! Chug it!

This science is so well accepted that it has in fact influenced not just our parenting styles but also our legal system. In 2005, the U.S. Supreme Court abolished the death penalty for crimes that had been committed by children under the age of eighteen. This ruling effectively delineated the legal line between adolescence and adulthood as eighteen—although we think, given that the average age when human brain development is complete is twenty-two, it didn't go quite far enough.

In the case of Alex, his parents had successfully established open and honest lines of communication that allowed them to sit down with Alex and present him with their real concerns about the hazards of young-adult drinking. They could each express their concerns, backed up by some indisputable facts, that could help temper and inform Alex's decision-making processes when he was confronted by unfamiliar or potentially dangerous emotional situations.

Of course, sitting down with anyone—teenager, young adult, or *old* adult—and simply presenting facts is not always the most efficient way to deliver information. Think of any dinner-party debate you've ever had with someone whose political position, for instance, differs from yours. You can present all the facts you want or have at hand, but if someone has been raised in a conservative home, he is likely to remain as conservative as when your conversation began, and someone who has been raised in a more liberal atmosphere is unlikely to change his mind, either. That's because their political affiliations provoke strong *emotions*—feelings of loyalty to family, party, or even a particular candidate. It's their emotions that are involved in their political decision-making process—"hot cognition" as opposed to a "cold" analysis of just the facts.

So while we recognize the core importance of the open communication between Alex and his parents and applaud it, we want to ask an even deeper question: What are the factors that enabled this sort of fluid and nonjudgmental exchange of information between parents and child in the first place? As we head into the next sections of this chapter, remember the words *attachment* and *modeling*—these are key concepts, and we are going to help define them for you by contrasting Alex's story with that of another child, Jacob.

Among his group of friends, Jacob was the designated buyer. That is, he was the one of his crew of nine-year-olds whose courage never failed him when he entered a pharmacy with the intention of purchasing a bottle or two of over-the-counter cough syrup. Jacob's friends would become intimidated if a pharmacist or a sales clerk questioned their purchase, but Jacob was able to coolly handle any inquiries, soberly make his purchase, and hold his laughter until he rejoined his friends outside the store.

There are over 125 brands of over-the-counter cough remedies and cold medications on the market that contain the drug dextromethorphan (DXM). DXM is a synthetic drug that produces a hallucinogenic effect when consumed in great enough quantities. And a growing number of children in the United States, some as young as Jacob at eight and nine years of age, are using it to get high. Indeed, nearly 10 percent of American teenagers have admitted to using it at least once.[12]

The kids call the practice of getting high on DXM "Robo tripping" and refer to the medications that contain the drug by a variety of names—"Robo," "Skittles," "Dex," and "Tussin." Robo tripping is a dangerous practice—it can lead from "mere" hallucinations to loss of motor control to death. Now, your first question might not be, What could provoke a child as young as eight or nine years old to do something so dangerous that has proven to be so fatal to so many children? But we all know that nine-year-olds don't have a well-developed sense of their own mortality, and they'd just as likely as not rush enthusiastically into many activities that would give a grown person pause—bungee jumping, say, or white-water rafting. The question that should occur to you is, *How deeply must a nine-year-old child be hurting to want to hallucinate his way out of his life for a while?* What factors are at work in his life that are leading him to indulge in this risky behavior? What is going on in his life—or what trauma has occurred in his life—that may be contributing to his taking his first steps on the road to becoming an addict?

The human brain is wondrously complex. Indeed, it is likely the most intricately formed system in the entire universe. It coordinates our movements so we can walk and talk, throw a football, play a guitar, or sing a song; it automates physical functions like our breathing, the beating of our heart, and the modulation of our body's temperature; it regulates how we experience our senses, feel heat, see light, and smell dinner cooking; it processes both outside stimuli and abstract concepts so we can make a joke, analyze a problem, or create a poem; and it captures, stores, and categorizes the memories of all our experiences so that when we recall these experiences, we can answer correctly on a test, recognize danger, or pine for a loved one who is far away—so we can, in short, attach appropriate emotions to the situations we encounter.

The incredible human brain does all of these things by way of electrical signals that travel cell to cell along what are called *neural pathways*. Neural pathways are, to put it in plain terms, the "grooves" that are worn in our brain through the process of learning. Whether what we are learning is our times tables in the second grade, how to solve an algebra problem when we are teenagers, or how to follow along as our accountant explains some intricacy of tax law to us, what we are doing when we incorporate a previously unknown bit of information into our repertoire is wearing a new neural pathway in our brain. These pathways are much like the lines that, in therapy, we want to create between the dots of experience and emotion. The neural pathways we are able to develop at any given stage of our lives depend on two factors—the maturity and health of our brain.

Most of us learn our times tables around the time we are six or seven years old because that is the stage of our lives when our brain has grown to the point where we are able to develop the neural pathways necessary to retain the fact that four times four equals sixteen. And while we wouldn't anticipate that the average six-year-old could make sense of an algebraic equation, we do expect a sixteen-year-old to be able to grasp algebraic concepts. Similarly, by the time we are grown enough to hold a full-time job and pay taxes, we are expected to be able to understand some basic concepts of the tax code in a way that will allow us to efficiently organize our financial lives. This is because as our brain grows and matures, the efficiency of the electrical signals in our brain increases. The efficiency is a matter of, in great part, a process called myelination,[13] during which a fatty sheath develops around the brain cells. Again, to put it in the simplest terms, this fatty sheath smoothes the path that the electricity must travel and tightens the connection between the cells.

Of course, it's not only math concepts that the brain grows increasingly able to absorb as it matures. A six-year-old can delight her family at a ballet recital, but she won't yet have the motor skills that would allow her to take a starring role in an American Ballet Theatre production of *Giselle*. She would have to work to train both her body and her *brain* for many years to work up to such a role—not only must she be able to perform the steps, but she must etch the grooves in her brain that allow her body to remember the steps.

Sadly, it is also true that a ballerina's ability to perform at her peak is limited. The aging body and the aging brain make the role progressively more difficult to execute—just as it becomes progressively more difficult for an aging brain to remember that four times four equals sixteen, remember where the car keys were placed, or remember what in the world was needed at the grocery store.

Having said these things—having recognized that the brain grows and flourishes, then withers and deteriorates as does any other biological component—we must also recognize that, like any other part of the body, the brain grows or deteriorates based on many factors, not simply the age or maturity of the organism that contains it. Take, for example, the femur, or the thigh bone, which can grow to up to more than eighteen inches long in an adult man, or about the whole length of the average newborn, and can deteriorate by way of diseases such as osteoporosis. Although osteoporosis is best known as an "old person's" disease, all old people don't get osteoporosis. Diet, exercise, environment, and genetics all play a role in determining the strength and health of the femur as the body ages. These same factors can help determine the ongoing health of the brain as it grows and ages, and scientists are also beginning to discover the crucial role of these factors, particularly environment and "brain exercise," in preventing or delaying the onset of the age-related neurological disease Alzheimer's as well.

But even more to the larger point we want to make is that, like the femur, the brain can repair itself when it is broken. The brain is not, as was once thought, a static system that changed little after the *critical period* of infancy. A critical period, in terms of developmental psychology and developmental biology, is a time frame in the early stages of an organism's life when it is most responsive to certain stimuli in its environment and develops in a way that is a specific response to the experience of these stimuli. The chaffinch, a small bird in the finch family, for example, must hear an adult bird sing during a critical period of its early life or it will never learn to sing the chaffinch's distinctive song.

The human brain is not quite so rigid about the periods of time during which it can learn to sing a new song, and this is due to a quality called *neuroplasticity*. Neuroplasticity, or plasticity, is the brain's lifelong ability to reorganize—to regenerate or to even create anew—its neural pathways based on new information and experiences. Think again, for a moment, of our illustration of a road map. Learning, as we've said, is the process of wearing neural pathways, or roads, along which electrical impulses can travel to store and retrieve the information we need every day—math skills to balance our checkbook, for example, or a memory that we call upon to inform how we will react in a similar emotional situation.

When we are young and learning a lesson for the first time or older and just beginning to learn a new skill or having a new experience for the very first time, we lay down the primary neural pathways in our brain that relate to that particular piece of information or skill set or memory. But the first time we recite the times tables, for example, we create a pathway that is no more than a dirt road. Repeating the tables—or practicing our golf swing or retelling a funny story that happened to us—improves the road, grading it, paving it, and, in some cases, turning it into a superhighway so we can retrieve the information we need handily and put it to use.

But what happens if we're driving in a car and the road we're traveling on is closed for some reason, whether it be due to construction or bad weather? We take a detour. We find another road on which to travel to our destination. The human brain has the same remarkable ability to make detours. It is a supremely adaptable mechanism that can relearn lost skills and functions, even to the point of, in some cases, being able to compensate for physical brain injury. Even after a person suffers a traumatic physical event such as a stroke, in which a part of the brain actually "dies" during the event, it is possible to retrain the neurons that remain alive to compensate for the loss. "It is not only the number of neurons that are left but how they function and what connections they can make that will decide the functional outcome."[14]

That is the upside of neuroplasticity—the brain's remarkable ability to heal itself or regain its functional balance.

To explain the downside, we want you to consider that damage to the brain occurs not only in the physical realm or in ways that are precisely measurable by the instruments and technologies currently at our disposal. We humans are able to process information and experiences in ways that create new neural pathways that are not always beneficial to us.

Take, for example, the experience of Lisa who, in her senior year of college, got engaged to the guy of her dreams—and then weeks before their scheduled wedding the August after graduation got dumped by him. This traumatic experience "taught" Lisa that she was unattractive, unworthy, and unlovable. Several years of instability—the inability to hold a job, risky promiscuity, and binge drinking—were, fortunately, followed by several years of therapy during which time Lisa was able to "relearn" her own worth.

Moreover, psychological disorders are, as we have said, the result of either the brain's organic biochemical malfunctions, such as in bipolar disorder or schizophrenia, or trauma that alters our brain chemistry and/or neural pathways. And, as we are focusing on children in this chapter, the burning question is, What happens to the *growing* brains of children who suffer from psychological disorders, whose developing brains are creating primary pathways in an unhealthy biochemical stew? Well, we don't have the answer yet—neuroscience is, in spite of all of its outstanding advances, in its infancy. But, for example, we do know that childhood anxiety has been linked with increased activity in certain areas of the brain. "We believe that young children who have higher activity in these brain regions are more likely to develop anxiety and depression as adolescents and adults, and are also more likely to develop drug and alcohol problems in an attempt to treat their distress,"[15] according to Dr. Ned H. Kalin, the chair of psychiatry at the University of Wisconsin–Madison School of Medicine and Public Health.

Research such as this raises the following question: Can we predict whether a child will have problems with drugs and alcohol? Yes, we believe that we can.

But understanding how the brain works—the ways in which it develops, as well as its extraordinary ability to restore itself—also tells us that we have the tools to prevent the damage from occurring or repair it once it has taken place.

The problem is, will those close to that child listen?

Jacob, the "Robo tripper" you read about earlier in this chapter, started to become a handful when he was around six years of age. He began sneaking out of the house at night, engaging in petty vandalism with a group of slightly older neighborhood kids. His teachers began suspending him from

school because he was verbally aggressive and used foul language in the classroom. His grades fell, and his mother found
cigarettes and marijuana, along with a lot of empty cough
syrup bottles, stashed in his closet. She had taken to hiding her purse from him because there were frequently small
amounts of money missing from it. Although she could never
catch him in the act of stealing, she could always trace an
empty wallet back to a point where Jacob had been alone in
a room with it. Around the neighborhood, Jacob began to be
known as a "bad seed."

For nearly three years, Jacob's family had begged his
mother to get him help—or at least to consult with his school's
psychologist about his increasingly unacceptable behavior.
And for nearly three years, Jacob's mother had enabled his
poor performance by dismissing it as "a phase" and "typical
all-boy behavior." Strange as this might sound, Jacob got
lucky and got caught when he tried to swipe some cash from
a neighbor's purse. Because the neighbor decided to press
charges, Jacob's mother was forced to confront the situation.
It didn't take many sessions for the psychiatrist with whom
Jacob had entered treatment to determine that he wasn't a
bad seed. What he was instead was depressed, suffering from
unresolved grief that had begun when his paternal grandfather, to whom he was very close, died suddenly. You won't
be surprised when we tell you that this death occurred when
Jacob was six years old or that, by dismissing Jacob's subsequent unacceptable and sometimes outrageous behaviors as
somehow typical for a growing boy, his mother had enabled
him to get away with his mistakes until he had really begun
to spiral out of control.

Long before the crisis of the theft, Jacob's family had
worn themselves out urging his mother to find a way to help

Jacob. And Jacob himself had been sending unmistakable signals that he needed and, indeed, *wanted* help. Children don't engage in continued extreme behaviors because those behaviors are pleasant; they act out because it is the only way that their still-unformed brains know to communicate some hidden and hurtful emotion. But the first thing we adults have to do is listen to them.

ANXIETY DISORDERS

Anxiety in childhood is normal in that most children will experience it to a greater or lesser degree at some stage. Some children may be shy around strangers or reluctant for a day or two to leave the safety of their familiar home for the new experience of school. These are typical phases of development and are temporary and harmless. A child may also see a television show or a movie that frightens him but quickly recover when a parent or older sibling reassures him that they understand he is afraid and reassure him again. This is also normal. It is when these phases are prolonged or when a child will not be comforted that the anxiety becomes an issue for real concern.

According to the Anxiety Disorders Association of American, one in eight children are affected by anxiety disorders, and anxiety disorders can often co-occur with other disorders such as eating disorders, depression, and ADHD.[16] As we discussed in our earlier section on adult anxiety, there are many ways that anxiety can manifest. GAD can show itself in a child who is constantly worried about her grades, her performance on sports teams, or how she fits in and is accepted by her peers. OCD usually shows up around the time a child is ten years old but has been diagnosed in children as young as two. PTSD is most prevalent in children who have suffered a critical emotional blow, such as the death of a parent; witnessed a traumatic event, such as a natural disaster; or been exposed to emotional, physical, or sexual abuse. Separation anxiety can be, as we've pointed out, a common and temporary phase of a child's life. Many children typically go through this stage when they are around a year and a half old, and it's not rare for a child who is a bit older to have a tough time leaving home on the first day or so of school. But when a child refuses to go to school or to a sleepover, or insists on someone staying with him at bedtime, then separation anxiety disorder must be considered. A child who suffers from this disorder is often reluctant to leave a parent or other caregiver because he fears that something terrible will happen to those people while he is absent.

Despite conceding that anxiety is common in childhood, however temporary and harmless, with statistics at 1 in 8, it is still far too prevalent—and it can be seen in the earliest stages in childhood. We propose that in the vast majority of cases, childhood anxiety can involve issues of attachment.

The primary "job" of the parent of a newborn is to keep that child alive and well. When a newborn enters the world, he is entirely dependent on others for his survival in the most literal sense. He cannot walk, talk, feed himself, or change his own diapers. The child's physical well-being—food, clothing, shelter, health care—is utterly in the hands of his parents.

To clarify, we use the term *parent* to also refer to significant others who play an ongoing and constant role in the newborn's life. These significant others can be a grandparent, an aunt or an uncle, siblings, or even a nurse or a nanny—anyone who has a strong emotional attachment and vesting with the infant. Although these others often assist with the day-to-day, hour-to-hour feeding and diapering, their strong emotional attachment to the infant is equally as important to the survival of the infant as the physical care he receives.

The definition of *attachment* is "connection by ties of affection and regard...a connection by which one thing is attached to another."[17] *Attachment theory* is a psychological theory about the relationships between humans. It was developed by the psychiatrist and psychoanalyst John Bowlby in the late 1960s, and its chief tenet is that an infant must develop a strong bond with at least one primary caregiver in order to develop socially and emotionally in a typical manner. The key factors in creating this bond are the following: The caregiver must be responsive and sensitive in interactions with the infant; the child must be able to consistently look to the caregiver to soothe him in times of stress (from changing his diaper when he is disturbed because it is wet to cuddling him when he is startled by a sudden noise); and the caregiver must remain as a constant in the child's life from the time the child is six months old to the time he is at least two years of age.

Anyone who has taken a beginning course in psychology in the last forty years has learned that attachment is a fundamental issue that determines whether the newborn infant *thrives*. This concept is often presented in the negative—that is, failure to thrive (FTT), which is a medical term used to describe poor physical growth. Poor care by an incompetent or apathetic caregiver, or from a mother who is herself suffering from debilitating postpartum depression, can result in children who are underweight, are developmentally delayed, and have notably poor postures.

The other way in which you can observe if an infant is thriving is if the infant's behavior is age appropriate. Is her demeanor sad or withdrawn? Conversely, is his demeanor hyperirritable and angry? Does he seek to make eye contact? Does she cry when she would be expected to cry? Does he follow people with his eyes and take an interest in what is happening around him? An important caveat, of course, is that these issues are present with an otherwise physically intact infant—in other words, the infant is physically and neurologically healthy. But even without measurable outward signs such as a failure to gain appropriate weight, negative answers to the last three questions in this paragraph, posed in reference to a neurotypical child, can be real warning signs of emotionally stunted development and danger on the road of life ahead.

*   *   *

Attachment theory is a school of thought in psychology about which volumes have been written; the psychological, evolutionary, and ethological aspects of the subject have been dissected in what are likely several hundred thousand pages. We cannot therefore do the subject justice in just one chapter, but we can present a glimpse of attachment issues as they pertain to substance use and abuse later in life. Even the simplified version we provide, however, can help with a better understanding of how critical attachment is to human well-being—and how the dots between early life and later-life issues are fatefully connected.

It has been well established and widely agreed upon that the "first five" years of a child's life determine her success in life, in school, in work, and in relationships. It is a fact most touted by educators who look to the importance of early education as a determinate of the child's later success in life. According to the United Nations Educational, Scientific and Cultural Organization (UNESCO), early childhood is defined as the period from birth to eight years. This international organization acknowledges that "the foundations of human development are laid during the child's early years,"[18] which are "a time of remarkable brain development,"[19] and that "early childhood care and education...is more than a preparatory stage assisting the child's transition to formal schooling. Today, early childhood policies are placed within a broader context of social development, gender equity and poverty reduction."[20]

We believe that the foundation for success in adult life occurs much earlier—in the first months and first years of the child's life—and that this foundation is formed in the child's attachment to her parents. The child who has a secure attachment to her parents is able to securely go out into the world. The child who does not have a secure attachment has difficulty entering the world; they are anxious, and they have difficulty relating and interacting with others. As we've noted, all children go through an adjustment phase when they begin the process of entering the world outside their home and family, but it is just that—a phase. The child who is securely attached is able to move through the phase, whereas the child who is insecurely attached does not. The insecure child can present as anxious, fearful and tearful, or withdrawn. Most people can spot a child who is struggling with attachment issues even though they cannot apply clinical terminology to what they see.

We were at a family dinner at a restaurant recently and noticed, a few tables away, another family there to celebrate a child's birthday. The birthday boy was about eight years old, and in spite of being surrounded by what appeared to be his whole loving extended family, the child would duck down under the table whenever the waitress arrived at the table. He wouldn't engage with her—not even when encouraged by family members to tell her if he wanted a Coke or a root beer with his dinner—and actually broke into wails when, later, it came time to order food and his mother pressed him to place the order himself. He was clearly terrified of this stranger—and in a manner that would have been extreme for even a much younger child. We've all witnessed some such scene—and possibly dismissed it as a temper tantrum or a shy child having a "bad day"—but to a trained eye, the deeper issues are all but written across the child's forehead.

Now, of course, it's not only observation or anecdotal evidence that we need rely on for confirmation of this theory. In 1997, a study was done with newborns to determine "whether infants who were anxiously/resistantly attached in infancy develop more anxiety disorders during childhood and adolescence than infants who were securely attached."[21] The infants who were the subjects of the study participated in the Ainsworth Strange Situation Procedure at the age of twelve months. The Ainsworth Strange Situation Procedure is a test developed by the researcher Mary Ainsworth in the 1970s from which she concluded that there were three major types of infant attachment: secure attachment, ambivalent-insecure attachment, and avoidant-insecure attachment.

The researchers then went on to complete a longitudinal study—that is, a study done over many years—that followed these infants and noted what, if any, issues developed by the time they were 17.5 years of age. Indeed, those newborns who had a difficult attachment with their mothers and were infants who seemed hard to soothe became children who appeared to be anxious or stressed as teenagers.[22]

You may be wondering why this information is presented in a book about addiction. The fact of the matter is that the majority of children who experience high levels of anxiety and stress will end up self-medicating with alcohol or drugs, sex or gambling, or some other addictive behavior to deal with their adult emotions. And the foundation for the adult anxiety and stress that they experience as being so painful they must be numbed begins in their first years of life. Earlier, we presented statistics about when children take their first drink or use over-the-counter medication; recall those numbers now and understand that the infant who has difficulty in attachment becomes the child who is anxious, who then becomes the youngster who tries alcohol and drugs at far too early an age, who then becomes the adult who struggles with a lifetime of addiction-related problems.

ADD/ADHD

According to the CDC, as of 2007, the number of children in the United States between the ages of four and seventeen who have been diagnosed with ADD/ADHD is 5.4 million— or 9.5 percent of that population—and the rate of diagnosis has been increasing by more than 3 percent every year since.[23] Would the number of children diagnosed with this disorder lessen if we began to look at the same children through the viewpoint of early attachment issues and anxiety? That is, the symptoms associated with this disorder are very real—just ask any public-school elementary educator— but as you'll see, the symptoms vary wildly and encompass both physical and psychological aspects, and the danger is that we are lumping several disorders with nuanced differences into one catchall term.

ADD (attention deficit disorder) and ADHD (attention deficit/hyperactivity disorder) are one and the same disorder—a disorder characterized by impulsivity, difficulty in concentrating or staying focused, an inability to stay seated, and periods of hyperactivity. But there is no one test that can be administered to achieve a diagnosis, nor is there one clear-cut list of symptoms that make a diagnosis of this disorder indisputable. Only two parameters, in fact, make the diagnosis just a bit less subjective: The characteristic symptoms of the disorder need to have been present for at least six months prior to diagnosis and the symptoms need to be manifest in at least two environments—at, say, both home and school—for a diagnosis to become official. But when medical tests have ruled out other physical issues for the symptoms, ADD/ADHD is, as of this writing, the most convenient label. We say "as of this writing" because research in this area is still ongoing, and every day we are learning more about the human brain and its evolution.

This is not to say that children who are diagnosed with ADD/ADHD or their parents don't suffer the grief or the real consequences of behavioral problems. It is to say that perhaps the diagnosis has become too commonplace or prevalent while effective treatment for a real and growing problem lags far behind the need.

But let's get beyond the issue of diagnosis for a moment and talk about what is more and more becoming a standard treatment in these cases: medication. As of 2007, 2.7 million children from the ages of four to seventeen with a current diagnosis of ADHD were receiving medication for the disorder.[24] Most commonly, the medicine prescribed in these cases is a stimulant, the most widely used being Ritalin, Adderall, and Dexedrine.

It might seem counterintuitive that a stimulant is commonly prescribed to treat a disorder that has hyperactivity as one of its defining features, so it's important to know how these drugs are supposed to work in the child's system: Stimulants are believed to be effective because they increase dopamine levels in the brain. Dopamine is a neurotransmitter associated with attention, and it is believed that increasing the amount of dopamine available to the ADHD child will improve his focus; almost by default, then, when focus is improved, hyperactivity and impulsivity will be reduced.

The advent of the use of medication to treat ADD and ADHD has made a real difference in the lives of some children and their ability to stay the course at school. With that we have no quarrel. However, the use of medication must be adopted within definite parameters—and with an understanding that there is a slippery slope ahead if the medication is used without the concurrent employment of traditional therapy to discern the core causes of the child's behavioral issues. Why?

Well, first of all, the use of medications to treat ADD and ADHD is on the rise, as is the abuse of these medications. The street sale and use of medication regularly prescribed to treat this disorder is prevalent and growing at an alarming rate. This is because this class of drugs produces a very pleasurable feeling in its users. The drugs work by increasing the amount of dopamine in the user's system, remember, and dopamine is associated not only with attention but also with pleasure. Like serotonin, it's part of the natural biochemical recipe for "happy juice." According to NIDA, America's children are getting very happy—this class of medication ranks third among twelfth graders for illicit drug use.[25] In fact, the effects of the drug are so pleasurable that some children—as well as some adults—actually try to fake the symptoms of ADHD in order to get a prescription for the drugs most commonly used to treat it.[26]

Second, we cannot give short shrift to the conditions that might well be *causing* ADHD. It is, for instance, important to understand the role that physical environment plays in the developing child's body. Some children are highly sensitive to environmental elements. For example, some children do not efficiently eliminate metals. Rather than excrete them as many children do, their bodies store them up, leading to a toxic biological environment that alters the child's body chemistry and hence their brain development and behavior. To illustrate, in 2004, researchers at the University of Texas Health Science Center in San Antonio did a study in which they compared the incidence of autism rates vis-à-vis the patients' long-term proximity to sites where mercury was routinely released into the environment—sites such as coal-burning power plants, for example. What they found was that for every 1,000 pounds of environmentally released mercury, there was a 61 percent increase in the autism rate in the immediate area.[27] We need similar studies to be undertaken to determine if mercury or the increasing release of other environmental toxins can be linked with not just the rise in autism rates but also the rise of ADD/ADHD and other childhood developmental disorders. When the cause is known, parents and health-care providers can better detect it in its formative stages, and steps can be taken to vastly reduce or eliminate the toxic effects on the child.

Another reason to be vigilant about how we proceed with the diagnosis and treatment of ADHD—and to clamor for studies that can reveal its cause—is its cost. The annual "cost of illness" for this disorder in the United States calculated in 2005 dollars was between $36 and $52 billion.[28] For each child who is afflicted, a family can expect to spend between $12,000 and $17,000 in health-care costs annually.[29] Across ten countries, it was projected that ADHD was associated with 143.8 million lost days of productivity each year.[30] Our children can't afford the physical and psychological costs of ADHD, and, as a nation, we can afford neither the loss of money nor the loss of the productivity and creativity of those who suffer with it.

Finally, we cannot stress too strongly that education experts have vastly improved the lives of many formerly unruly and dissatisfied children with the diagnosis of and intervention for—particularly *early* diagnosis and intervention—learning issues and disabilities. Children who were previously thought to be poor students because of a lack of motivation or desire, or the inability to stay seated and stay focused, have found great success in education and life through the proper identification of their learning needs. Children with learning disorders understand, remember, and respond to new information in ways that are different from neurotypical children. Common learning disabilities revolve around the inability to read and write, do math, express oneself verbally, and pay attention. Tellingly, about one-third of children who have been diagnosed with a learning disability have also been diagnosed with ADHD.

The baseline, however, is that the use of medication to treat ADD/ADHD can be quite effective in soothing the symptoms of this disorder, but it is best used in combination with verbal intervention, especially in those instances when there is no clear biological underpinning for the diagnosis. This means working with the child to identify the triggers that lead him to feel a lack of focus, an inability to pay attention or to sit still, and then giving that child the tools to use to modify his own behavior when those situations arise. This approach is very time and attention intensive; both the child's parents and his teachers must work in partnership with the student on an ongoing basis. But when the effort is invested, it can lead to real, substantive behavioral changes without the ongoing use of medication or even without any medication at all. And this success can be transferred to other areas in the child's life—the ability to calm himself down, to de-stress when faced with an anxiety-provoking situation—and can have a long-term impact. Giving a child a pill may make him sit still in class for a day, but giving him back control over his own behaviors will serve him for a lifetime.

SOCIETAL AND PARENTAL MODELING

A friend recently cut short a lunch date because she was leaving for a two-week vacation in Hawaii the next day. She wasn't worried about getting home to pack—the packing was nearly complete—but she was frantic to make sure that she got to the pharmacy in time to pick up her prescription. She needed a sedative because she was afraid of flying, because she had a hard time sleeping in strange hotel beds, because her husband was taking her deep-sea fishing and she was terrified of open water, because she didn't want to fret the whole time she was away about the children at home with the sitter, and so on. She was experiencing so much high anxiety that you sort of had to feel sorry for her having to spend two weeks in the sunshine on a white-sand beach. Her prescription was in hand, however, and she was quite looking forward to the trip.

It is important to note that the use of medication to treat emotional issues sets up a paradigm that you can take a pill to feel differently. Our friend in Hawaii was deeply dependent on chemical happiness. As we pointed out in the section on the use of medication to treat children with ADD/ADHD, there is a slippery slope that leads to the misuse of medication. The friend who needs a pile of pills in order to enjoy her vacation can too easily become the friend who needs a pile of pills in order to get through her daily life without crushing anxiety.

The child who is highly anxious at school may indeed benefit from a short and specific course of medication to calm her down and allow her to experience less anxiety while at school. In theory, when she is able to experience less anxiety in a given situation that previously led to very high levels of anxiety, she can more effectively engage in progressive communication and problem solving. And the way to achieve this lessened anxiety state is sometimes through medication. Similarly, our friend might have fared better on her white-sand beach had she relied on her medications not to contain her fears but only to allay them while she worked with a therapist to get to the root of why she hated to get on an airplane or go out on a boat, or why she obsessed about what she thought would happen to her children while she was away from them and they were in the care of a long-trusted babysitter.

The danger, you see, is that a person will feel that, in order to calm down, she must *always* take the medication.

The medication becomes a crutch, and the happiness, calm, or sense of well-being the person experiences while using it is not authentic. That is because the primary problem in using medication in this way is that the locus of control is not within the person; rather, it is external. The control is accessible only through a prescription bottle, and therefore the person does not feel that she can effect change within herself to feel better or more comfortable. Again, we come to the slippery slope: The individual, whether a child or an adult, "learns" that she needs medication in order to feel better emotionally. This then sets up the connection in the person's mind that she can use medication to "fix" all of her problems. Anything that makes her uncomfortable, anxious, sad, or fearful becomes an occasion to take a pill.

OR A DRINK.
OR A LINE.
OR A HIT.

The fact of the matter is that the same results of lessening a child's anxiety can very often be achieved without the use of medication. There are, of course, exceptions to this rule, but they are by far a minority of cases. And the plain fact of the matter is that to achieve the desired results with or without meds takes time, attention, and cooperation—parents and educators working in partnership and with dedication to the child's well-being.

As you read this, you may be thinking that we are moving into the realm of a parenting book. While there is some validity to that supposition, there is also a valid reason to present this information in this context. Dr. Karen gives talks at schools in our local area, and the talk that she gives to parents of elementary school–aged children frequently makes her an unpopular adult on campus. This talk revolves around educating parents in the art of raising children who are addiction free, and, essentially, she tells parents that they aren't going to be able to make a good job of it if they are modeling drinking or prescription-drug-abuse behaviors to their children.

And often, simply because of the culture that we live in, this is exactly what they are doing.

Now, "modeling" is not a new concept. It has long been agreed upon that if we model good behavior to our children—if we look both ways when crossing in the crosswalk, obey the rules of the road while we're driving, wear a helmet while we're biking—then our children will adopt these good habits and behaviors. "Do as I say, not as I do" is a risky motto when it comes to child rearing; your children will do as you *do*. If you behave conscientiously, this is the behavior your children will mirror. When you obey the rules set by your boss or your homeowners' association or your local traffic cop and the larger society in general, your children learn to obey the rules the teacher sets in the classroom—and that you set at home. Your child's budding sense of responsibility is reinforced by the responsible actions he sees around him on a daily basis.

Parents also, alas, model drinking and in the most insidious but seemingly innocent ways. Ask yourself the following questions:

- Do I ever have a party or get-together where alcohol is *not* part of the festivities?
- Do I drink more than a few times a week?

- Do I say (to myself or others) any of the following?
  - "It's been a hard day; I need a drink."
  - "It's time to celebrate; I deserve a drink."
  - "It's cocktail time!"
  - "It's the weekend."
  - "It's five o'clock somewhere."
  - "I'm on vacation!"
  - "I didn't get to go on vacation so I ought to do *something* to relax."

For the most part, in this culture, drinking is a part of our socializing. Think about how we celebrate: champagne on birthdays and anniversaries, beer at football games, spiked eggnog at winter holiday parties, margaritas at backyard barbecues, and so on. Alcohol is almost always involved in these occasions. It is likely, in fact, that our children rarely see us having a good time with family and friends *unless* we have something alcoholic in our hands. If that's not modeling drinking, what is?

Combine that startling realization with the fact that drinking alcohol is portrayed in the media as the thing to do. Simply watch a teen or even a preteen show and you either see or hear references to "getting wasted." The plots frequently revolve around one of the characters partying. According to a report done by the Institute of Alcohol Studies, "The characters used alcohol to help them enjoy dates and to celebrate special occasions. Even when characters were not explicitly drinking, alcohol appeared in the background—on shelves at the bar, on other tables in restaurants."[31] The teens in *Gossip Girl* "drink (and are served alcohol in bars)."[32] The kids on *Glee* can sing and dance—and drink and smoke.[33] There is even—however "unofficial" and surely unsanctioned by the network—a Hannah Montana drinking game.[34] In such ways, the presence of alcohol—and drinking it—becomes normalized.

Now add in the undeniable truth that we live in a culture that promotes the use of medications in the daily run of things. If you sit down and watch television for even a few hours, you will quickly notice the frequent ads for medications to treat anything that ails you, from gas and bloating to headaches and allergies and toenail fungus, from menstrual cramps and erectile dysfunction to shyness and sadness. There is no issue too big or too small that, it seems, can't be dealt with by doing anything more difficult than beating a trail to your doctor's office for a prescription.

Then, if you watch the television long enough, you will see that in the latter part of the day, the ads for alcohol begin. Frequently, these ads feature a celebrity promoting a lifestyle—Sean "Puffy" Combs for Cîroc vodka, Zach Galifianakis for Absolut vodka, Will Ferrell for Bud Light. For those of you old enough to remember cigarette ads, you will quickly catch on to the train of thought here. Before cigarette ads were taken off television and before it became politically incorrect to show a star smoking as part of the scene, smoking was part of the script. Frank Sinatra puffing away while he sang or Rob Petrie chivalrously lighting Laura's Kent cigarette—this was part of our indoctrination to the culture of smoking. Today, our children are being indoctrinated in the use of alcohol and prescription drugs. They are presented as both Band-Aids and cure-alls. But once a person begins to use medications—and make no mistake: Cîroc vodka is as much of a medication as Adderall—to change how he feels, he is already losing his footing on that slippery slope that leads to addiction to substances to get through everyday life.

People Who Come from Families of Addiction

Dad has a martini, or three, before dinner every night. Mom smokes cigarettes and has a prescription for an antianxiety med. Junior is on Ritalin. Grandpa spends most evenings glued to his computer screen looking at porn sites.

Family history is a factor that predisposes an individual to addiction. All of us know families that have multiple members who have drug and alcohol problems; the actual statistics are—well, *sobering*: "Biological children of alcohol dependent parents who have been adopted continue to have an increased risk (2–9 fold) of developing alcoholism."[35] "Use of substances by parents and their adolescent children is strongly correlated; generally, if parents take drugs, sooner or later their children will also. Adolescents who use drugs are more likely to have one or more parents who also use drugs."[36]

The largest part of this can be explained by modeling. A parent is both a guardian and a guide—the driver of the family car, so to speak; when the person who is driving the car takes a wrong turn on the wrong road, it is almost impossible to expect that the child will end up at a different destination.

But the question has long been posed about whether or not there is also a hereditary issue at work: Is alcohol or drug abuse learned, or is there a genetic predisposition as well?

Because the pattern of addiction runs "in the family," researchers have long attempted to find a gene for addiction or alcoholism—which has been dubbed in the media as the "alcoholism gene"—but if it does exist, it is proving to be elusive. For many years, there have been studies done to try to isolate this gene, but none has been successful up to this point.

Keep in mind, however, that addiction is a complicated disease. For example, "some thirty to seventy percent of alcoholics are reported to suffer from anxiety and depression,"[37] notes Subhash C. Pandey, a neuroscientist at the University of Illinois at Chicago. His work has therefore been focused on the CREB[38] gene that is involved in both the body's response to anxiety and the body's tolerance for alcohol.

Addiction is multifaceted; there is physical addiction, emotional addiction, and habit formation. There is anxiety, and there is, possibly, a genetic factor in the tolerance that anxious people have for alcohol. While researchers have not yet found an "alcoholism gene," we don't rule out its existence. But Dr. Pandey's work goes to what is really the larger point: Even if there were a drug that effectively removed the physical addiction, the other issues—the emotional addiction; the habit; and, indeed, the anxiety—would remain.

Is there an answer to the age-old question of learned versus inherited, nature versus nurture? In the case of addiction, we don't know if the world will ever really get it settled once and for all.

But we do know this: When we are asked if we can predict which kids are more likely to use drugs and alcohol when they grow up and which kids have a bigger chance than average of abusing these substances and becoming addicted to them, we answer that yes, we can. And it's mostly a matter of simple observation: How does the child behave? How do the parents behave? How do the parents and child interact? We take these few pieces of information, and then we connect the dots.

CONCLUSION

The Tyranny of Now

*I*N 1999, A book called *The Power of Now: A Guide to Spiritual Enlightenment*, written by Eckhart Tolle, was published. The core message of this book is that by deeply embracing the present moment, a person can learn to accept life as it is—that when we learn to stop resisting our reality, we can come to a place of peace, stillness, and joy.

This is a beautiful message—and one that has touched the lives of a great many: The book has sold over three million copies worldwide. For people suffering with addictive behaviors and for their loved ones, this message of living in "the now" can have a special resonance. Truly accepting the realities of addiction makes it impossible for the addict to continue excusing his own unacceptable behaviors—and it makes it impossible for those who love him to continue enabling those behaviors. The unconditional embrace of the problem is one of the earliest and most powerful stops along the road to recovery.

But empowering as this idea is, Tolle has chosen to tell only half of the story; as with any powerful force, "the now" has its dark side, too.

We live in a culture in which everything moves *fast*. Communication, thanks to new technologies, is nearly instantaneous; indeed, many young people have never experienced the real pleasure of going to the mailbox and finding a long handwritten note from a faraway friend or relative. Entertainment and diversion are constantly available; just a generation ago, Charlie Brown and the Great Pumpkin were once-a-year visitors, and the whole family had to gather in front of the television set at promptly 7:30 on the evening the special aired or they'd have to wait another twelve months to see it. Now any movie, television show, piece of music, or electronic game is accessible 24/7 with just a couple of clicks on the computer. In 1968, McDonald's opened its one thousandth outlet; now there are over thirty thousand McDonald's franchises in the United States alone. Even our food is *fast*. We live in a world of immediately, without further delay, ASAP, at once, pronto! God, give me patience, and give it to me *now*!

Worse, we often think of people who don't have to wait to obtain the things they want as highfliers—wildly successful individuals who, in our culture, we are schooled to regard as enviable, even admirable. We, too, might fantasize about having a staff that jumps to fulfill our every whim. Angelina Jolie has just to think about traveling across the globe and her handlers make it happen; Donald Trump probably never has to ask twice for a cup of coffee before it's served to him just as he likes it; our boss wants it yesterday, and we give it to him. Wouldn't it be nice if we could live like that for awhile ourselves?

As a society, we have fallen prey to the tyranny of instant gratification. We like our instant messaging, drive-through burgers, and quick fixes. Instead of viewing our demanding boss as a person who probably has poor impulse control, we simply work faster, harder, and longer in the hopes of someday being in a position to get his job.

But when it comes to addiction, there are no quick fixes. Indeed, it goes right to our point, we think, that the name of a synthetic urine product designed to enable addicts to pass drug-screening tests is in fact "Quick Fix."[1] But beyond synthetic urine, there are no instantaneous, one-size-fits-all answers to overcoming addiction. There is no one pill to take that can restore a physiological system that is chemically out of balance. There is no one-hour session with even the most magical therapist that can cut to the heart of pain and despair and bring instant relief. The sort of pain that leads to addiction is accumulated over a lifetime. Helping a patient find the root of that pain and learn new, healthier behaviors to deal with it takes time.

The challenge for society in truly adopting this patient, multifaceted approach is that it must relinquish its obsession with easy answers.

Let's go back to the road trip we started at the very beginning of this book. Depending on the itinerary you set at the outset of such a trip, it can take days, weeks, or even months to travel from the shores of the Atlantic to the Pacific coast. You could, of course, break the speed limits all along the way and make record time in getting to your destination. But traveling in that manner includes the chance of getting a lot of expensive speeding tickets and the risk of motor vehicle accidents. And it also includes missing a lot of stops along the way. It would be hard to say that you have really seen the United States if all you have taken in is the same dull gray asphalt that lies all along I-90.

It is impossible to speed along the road to authentic recovery. The stops along the way, the psychic detours into memory, are the whole point of the trip. They are what connect our past experiences with our future behaviors, and so, it is in coming to terms with these memories that gives the trip meaning. It is only through knowing where we have been that we can truly know where we are. If the mental states we have lived through are obscured by pain and trauma—as well as, often, by biochemical imbalance—the place we *are* will always seem murky and bleak. The patient process of revisiting these states, of acknowledging, embracing, and forgiving the pain and trauma, is the only genuine way to take control of the way forward.

Notes

CHAPTER 1   Reframing the Vocabulary of Addiction

1. Drug Rehabs web site, http://www.alcohol-drug-treatment.net.
2. National Institutes of Health (NIH): National Institute on Alcohol Abuse and Alcoholism, "Alcoholism," MedlinePlus, http://www.nlm.nih.gov/medlineplus/alcoholism.html.
3. The Washington Informer, July 15, 2010, http://www .washingtoninformer.com/index.php?option=com_content&view =article&id=4085:obama-drug-czar-says-drug-addiction-is-a -health-problem&catid=50:local&Itemid=113.
4. Minnesota Department of Human Services, "Compulsive Gambling," http://www.dhs.state.mn.us/main/idcplg?IdcService =GET_DYNAMIC_CONVERSION&RevisionSelectionMethod =LatestReleased&dDocName=id_008574.
5. The Society for the Advancement of Sexual Health, http://www .sash.net/.
6. The U.S. Census Bureau estimated that the United States entered 2010 with a population of 308,400,408. This is the last year for which statistics are available. Citation: http://www.pbs .org/newshour/rundown/2010/01/census-308400408-americans -to-start-2010.html.
7. The 12 Steps, "Step 11," http://www.12step.org/the-12-steps/step -11.html.
8. Kathy P., "Sober Traveling: AA Roadside Assistance for a Recovering Alcoholic," *Los Angeles Times*, January 2, 2001.
9. Soram Khalsa, "What You Can Do about the Vitamin D Epidemic," *The Huffington Post*, http://www.huffingtonpost.com /dr-soram-khalsa/what-you-can-do-about-the_b_203600.html.
10. Candance B. Pert, *Molecules of Emotion: The Science Behind Mind-Body Medicine* (New York: Simon and Schuster, 1999).
11. Candace Pert, official web site, http://www.candacepert.com /index.html.

12. S. C. Roesch, and J. H. Amirkham, "Boundary Conditions for Self-Serving Attributions," *Journal of Applied Social Psychology* 27 (1997), 245–261.

CHAPTER 2   The First Dot

1. National Institute of Mental Health (NIMH), "The Numbers Count: Mental Disorders in America," http://www.nimh.nih .gov/health/publications/the-numbers-count-mental-disorders -in-america/index.shtml#MajorDepressive.
2. G. Dawson, S. B. Ashman, and L. J. Carver, "The Role of Early Experience in Shaping Behavioral and Brain Development and Its Implication for Social Policy," *Development and Psychology*, 12 (2000): 695–712.
3. Mental Health: A Report of the Surgeon General, http://www. surgeongeneral.gov/library/mentalhealth/chapter3/sec6.html.

CHAPTER 4   The Story of an Almost Addict

1. Centers for Disease Control and Prevention (CDC), "Alcohol and Public Health," http://www.cdc.gov/alcohol/faqs.htm #drinkingProblem.

CHAPTER 5   Trauma Survivors

1. Helen Davey, "The Effects of the Trauma of September 11," Self Psychology Page, http://www.selfpsychology.com/papers/davey _2002a_flight_attendants.htm.
2. R. C. Kessler, A. Sonnega, E. Bromet, M. Hughes, and C. B. Nelson, "Posttraumatic Stress Disorder in the National Comorbidity Survey," *Archives of General Psychiatry* 52, no. 12 (1995), http://www.ncbi.nlm.nih.gov/pubmed/7492257.
3. Sean Callebs, "Divorce Stalks Katrina Survivors," *CNN Living*, August 29, 2008, http://articles.cnn.com/2008-08-29/living/broken.homes. katrina_1_fema-trailer-divorce-gustav/2?_s=PM:LIVING.

4. Nicole LaPorte, "The Katrina Divorces," *Daily Beast*, August 22, 2010, http://www.thedailybeast.com/blogs-and-stories/2010-08 -22/hurricane-katrina-divorces-improve-couples-lives/.
5. Ibid.
6. B. Ganzel, B. J. Casey, G. Glover, H. U. Voss, and E. Temple, "The Aftermath of 9/11: Effect of Intensity and Recency of Trauma on Outcome," *Emotion* 7, no. 2 (2007), http://www.ncbi .nlm.nih.gov/pubmed/17516802.

CHAPTER 6   People with Anxiety Disorders

1. W. Lee and M. Hotopf, "Is Some Anxiety Good for You?," at Society of Personality and Social Psychology (Austin, TX: 2004).
2. Ibid.
3. David H. Zald, Mathew C. Hagen, and José V. Pardo, "Neural Correlates of Tasting Concentrated Quinine and Sugar Solutions," *Journal of Neurophysiology* 87, no. 2 (2002), http: //jn.physiology.org/cgi/content/full/87/2/1068; A. Etkin, K. E. Prater, A. F. Schatzberg, V. Menon, and M. D. Greicius, "Disrupted Amygdalar Subregion Functional Connectivity and Evidence of a Compensatory Network in Generalized Anxiety Disorder," *Archives of General Psychiatry* 66, no. 12 (2009), http: //www.ncbi.nlm.nih.gov/pubmed/19996041.
4. Zald, Hagen, and Pardo, "Neural Correlates."
5. B. H. Harvey, F. Oosthuizen, L. Brand, G. Wegener, and D. J. Stein, "Stress-Restress Evokes Sustained iNOS Activity and Altered GABA Levels and NMDA Receptors in Rat Hippocampus," *Psychopharmacology* 175, no. 4 (2004), http: //www.ncbi.nlm.nih.gov/pubmed/15138761.
6. Ibid.
7. HealthyPlace.com, "Anxiety Disorders Statistics and Facts," February 18, 2007, http://www.healthyplace.com/anxiety-panic /main/anxiety-disorders-statistics-and-facts/menu-id-69/.
8. Mental Health America, "Panic Disorder," http://www.nmha. org/go/panic-disorder.
9. Anxiety Disorders Association of America, "Facts & Statistics," http://www.adaa.org/about-adaa/press-room/facts-statistics.
10. Katherine Shear, Robert Jin, Ayelet Meron Ruscio, Ellen E. Walters, and Ronald C. Kessler, "Prevalence and Correlates of

Estimated DSM-IV Child and Adult Separation Anxiety Disorder in the National Comorbidity Survey Replication," *American Journal of Psychiatry* 163 (June 2006), http://ajp.psychiatryonline.org/cgi/content/full/163/6/1074.

11. Ibid., p. 1078.

12. Ibid.

13. National Institute of Mental Health (NIMH), "The Numbers Count: Mental Disorders in America," http://www.nimh.nih.gov/health/publications/the-numbers-count-mental-disorders-in-america/index.shtml#Social.

14. R. C. Kessler, P. Berglund, O. Demler, R. Jin, and E. E. Walters, "Lifetime Prevalence and Age-of-Onset Distributions of DSM-IV Disorders in the National Comorbidity Survey Replication," *Archives of General Psychiatry* 62 (2005), 593–602.

15. Karina Blair, Jonathan Shaywitz, Bruce W. Smith, Rebecca Rhodes, Marilla Geraci, Matthew Jones, Daniel McCaffrey, and others, "Response to Emotional Expressions in Generalized Social Phobia and Generalized Anxiety Disorder: Evidence for Separate Disorders," *American Journal of Psychiatry* 165 (2008), http://ajp.psychiatryonline.org/cgi/content/abstract/165/9/1193.

16. Jeremy D. Coplan, Susan I. Wolk, and Donald F. Klein, "Anxiety and the Serotonin$_{1A}$ Receptor," in *Psychopharmacology—4th Generation of Progress*, ed. Floyd E. Bloom and David J. Kupfer (Nashville, TN: American College of Neuropsychopharmacology, 2000), http://www.acnp.org/g4/GN401000125/CH123.html.

17. National Institute of Mental Health, "The Numbers Count."

18. Ibid.

19. Current Perspectives on Posttraumatic Stress Disorder: From the Clinic and the Laboratory, Stephen R. Paige, Department of Psychology, University of Nebraska at Omaha, http://www.icisf.org/articles/acrobat%20documents/terrorismincident/psytrauptsd.pdf.

20. P. E. Greenberg, T. Sisitsky, R. C. Kessler, S. N. Finkelstein, E. R. Berndt, J. R. Davidson, J. C. Ballenger, and A. J. Fyer, "The Economic Burden of Anxiety Disorders in the 1990s," *Journal of Clinical Psychiatry* 60, no. 7 (1999), http://www.ncbi.nlm.nih.gov/pubmed/10453795.

21. Catherine Valenti, "Are You Suffering from Vacation Deprivation?," *ABC News*, June 25, 2010, http://abcnews.go.com/Business/story?id=86551&page=1.

22. Ibid

23. Ibid.

24. Lyle H. Miller and Alma Dell Smith, *The Stress Solution: An Action Plan to Manage the Stress in Your Life* (New York: Pocket Books, 1993).

25. American Psychological Association, "Mind/Body Health: Did You Know?," http://www.apa.org/helpcenter/mind-body.aspx.

26. American Academy of Family Physicians, http://www.apa.org /helpcenter/mind-body.aspx.

27. American Psychological Association, "Mind/Body Health: Did You Know?"

28. Robert D. Stolorow, "Collective Trauma and Existential Anxiety," *The Huffington Post*, August, 13, 2010, http://www.huffingtonpost .com/robert-d-stolorow/collective-trauma-and-exi_b_680945 .html.

29. K. S. Kendler, T. J. Gallagher, J. M. Abelson, and R. C. Kessler, "Lifetime Prevalence, Demographic Risk Factors, and Diagnostic Validity of Nonaffective Psychosis as Assessed in a US Community Sample," The National Comorbidity Survey, *Archives of General Psychiatry*, 53 (1996): 1022–1031.

30. Sir Francis Bacon, *Religious Meditations, Of Heresies* (1597).

CHAPTER 7   Bipolar Disorder

1. S. Nassir Ghaemi, "Bipolar Disorder," Families for Depression Awareness, http://web.archive.org/web/20061207224847/http: //www.familyaware.org/expertprofiles/drghaemi4.asp.

2. World Health Organization, http://www.who.int/healthinfo /statistics/bod_bipolar.pdf

3. National Institute of Mental Health (NIMH), http://www.nimh .nih.gov/research-funding/scientific-meetings/2009/bipolar -disorder-in-children-and-adolescents-new-data-to-inform -classification/index.shtml.

4. Ibid.

5. Surgeon General's Report for Mental Health, http://www .surgeongeneral.gov/library/mentalhealth/chapter4/sec3_2 .html.

6. Richard B. Elsberry, "'Bipolar Disorder': Why Are They Calling It the 'CEO's Disease'?," *Electrical Apparatus*, February

1998, http://findarticles.com/p/articles/mi_qa3726/is_199802/ai_n8798710/.

7. National Institute of Mental Health (NIMH), "The Numbers Count: Mental Disorders in America," http://www.nimh.nih.gov/health/publications/the-numbers-count-mental-disorders-in-america/index.shtml#Bipolar.

8. Alan I. Leshner, "Drug Abuse and Mental Disorders: Comorbidity Is Reality," *NIDA Notes* 14, no. 4 (1999), http://archives.drugabuse.gov/NIDA_Notes/NNVol14N4/DirRepVol14N4.html.

9. Marcia Purse, "Dual Diagnosis: Is there a Single Cause?", October 29, 2009, http://bipolar.about.com/od/alcoholsubstanceabuse/a/aa010514a.htm.

10. *Diagnostic and Statistical Manual of Mental Disorders*, published by the American Psychiatric Association to provide a common language and standard criteria for diagnosing mental disorders; the most recent edition was produced in 2000.

11. W. Mansell and R. Pedley, "The Ascent into Mania: A Review of Psychological Processes Associated with the Development of Manic Symptoms," *Clinical Psychology Review* 28, no. 3 (2008), http://www.ncbi.nlm.nih.gov/pubmed/17825463.

12. Ronald C. Kessler, Katherine A. McGonagle, Shanyang Zhao, Christopher B. Nelson, Michael Hughes, Suzann Eshleman, Hans-Ulrich Wittchen, and Kenneth S. Kendler, "Lifetime and 12-Month Prevalence of DSM-III-R Psychiatric Disorders in the United States," *Archives of General Psychiatry* 51, no. 1 (1994), http://archpsyc.ama-assn.org/cgi/content/abstract/51/1/8.

13. Mauricio Tohen, Carlos A. Zarate, Jr., John Hennen, Hari-Mandir Kaur Khalsa, Stephen M. Strakowski, Priscilla Gebre-Medhin, Paola Salvatore, and Ross J. Baldessarini, "The McLean-Harvard First-Episode Mania Study: Prediction of Recovery and First Recurrence," *American Journal of Psychiatry* 160 (December 2003), http://ajp.psychiatryonline.org/cgi/content/full/160/12/2099.

CHAPTER 8   Depression and Addiction

1. J. R. Lacasse and J. Leo, "Serotonin and Depression: A Disconnect between the Advertisements and the Scientific Literature," *PLoS*

Medicine 2, no. 12 (2005), http://www.plosmedicine.org/article /info%3Adoi%2F10.1371%2Fjournal.pmed.0020392.

2. "About Lexapro: Lexapro Side Effects," Lexapro, http://www .lexapro.com/about-lexapro/lexapro-side-effects.aspx.

3. Ibid.

4. "Important Risk Information," Lexapro, http://www.lexapro .com/isi.aspx.

5. Liz Szabo, "Number of Americans Taking Antidepressants Doubles," *USA Today*, August 3, 2009, http://www.usatoday .com/news/health/2009-08-03-antidepressants_N.htm?csp=34.

6. Ibid.

7. Marilyn Elias, "Study: Most Depressed Kids Get Antidepressants but No Therapy," *USA Today*, October 8, 2008, http://www .usatoday.com/news/health/2008–10-08-kids-antidepressants -therapy_N.htm.

8. American Advertising Federation, "DTC Prescription Drug Advertising," http://www.aaf.org/default.asp?id=248.

9. M. S. Wilkes, R. A. Bell, and R. L. Kravitz, "Direct-to-Consumer Prescription Drug Advertising: Trends, Impact, and Implications," *Health Affairs* 19, no. 2 (2000), http://content.healthaffairs.org /cgi/reprint/19/2/110.

10. Charles Barber, *Comfortably Numb: How Psychiatry Is Medicating a Nation* (New York: Pantheon, 2008).

11. WebMD, "Causes of Depression," http://www.webmd.com /depression/guide/causes-depression.

12. Tori DeAngelis, "When Anger's a Plus," *Monitor* 34, no. 3 (2003), http://www.apa.org/monitor/mar03/whenanger.aspx.

13. Ibid.

CHAPTER 9   Children on the Slippery Slope

1. University of Connecticut, "Anti Hazing," http://www.greeklife .uconn.edu/hazing_stats.html.

2. Ibid.

3. Samuel Kuperman, Grace Chan, John R. Kramer, Laura Bierut, Kathleen K. Bucholz, Victor Hesselbrock, John I. Nurnberger, Jr., Theodore Reich, Wendy Reich, and Marc A. Schuckit, "Relationship of Age of First Drink to Child Behavioral Problems

and Family Psychopathology," *Alcoholism, Clinical and Experimental Research* 29, no. 10 (2005), http://www.stat.uiowa.edu/techrep/tr342.pdf.

4. American Academy of Pediatrics, "90% of Teens 'Wait' until after Age 11 for First Drink: AAP Poll," *AAP News* 14, no. 10 (1998), http://aapnews.aappublications.org/cgi/content/abstract/14/10/23.

5. Alcoholics Info, "What Are Alcoholics?," http://www.alcoholics-info.com/. The National Center on Addiction and Substance Abuse at Columbia University, 2005 Annual Report, "Planting the Seed for Our Children's Drug-Free Future."

6. Ibid.

7. Ibid.

8. Relationship of Age of First Drink to Child Behavioral Problems and Family Psychopathology, Samuel Kuperman, M.D., et al 2005.

9. Ibid.

10. http://physiciansforhumanrights.org/juvenile-justice/factsheets/braindev.pdf, "The Prefrontal Cortex—An Update: Time Is of the Essence," Joaquin M. Fuster, Neuropsychiatic Institute and Brain Research Institute, University of California, Los Angeles.

11. Ibid.

12. http://www.lifelinetomodernmedicine.com/ArticlePage.aspx?ID=48add67d-6283-42b3-b682-52000c91931e&LandingID=fc6eb1da-98e4-43c7-bb9f-09c17e2a005d. Letter to the Editor authored by faculty in the Center for Interventions and Addictions Research was printed in the November 2006 issue of *Pediatrics*, the official journal of the American Academy of Pediatrics. The entire letter is reprinted below or can be accessed through the journal's web site, http://www.med.wright.edu/citar/dads/letter.html. *Pediatrics* 118 (2006): 2267–2269.

13. Francine M. Benes, "Brain Development, VII: Human Brain Growth Spans Decades," *American Journal of Psychiatry* 155 (November 1998), http://ajp.psychiatryonline.org/cgi/content/full/155/11/1489.

14. Barbro B. Johansson, "Brain Plasticity and Stroke Rehabilitation: The Willis Lecture," *Stroke* 31 (2000), http://www.julieekstrum.com/japan/References/S.2000.31.1.223.pdf.

15. Jessica Ward Jones, "Anxiety Linked to Brain Activity," PsychCentral, http://psychcentral.com/news/2010/08/14/anxiety-linked-to-brain-activity/16823.html.

16. Anxiety Disorders Association of America, "Children," http://www.adaa.org/living-with-anxiety/children.

17. Webster's Dictionary.

18. United Nations Educational, Scientific and Cultural Organization (UNESCO), "Mission," http://www.unesco.org/en/early-childhood/mission/.

19. United Nations Educational, Scientific and Cultural Organization (UNESCO), "Early Childhood Care and Education," http://www.unesco.org/en/early-childhood/.

20. UNESCO, "Mission."

21. Susan L. Warren, Lisa Huston, Byron Egeland, and L. Alan Sroufe, abstract to "Child and Adolescent Anxiety Disorders and Early Attachment," *Journal of the American Academy of Child and Adolescent Psychiatry* 36, no. 5 (1997), http://www.jaacap.com/article/S0890-8567(09)62830-6/abstract.

22. Ibid.

23. Centers for Disease Control and Prevention (CDC), "Attention-Deficit / Hyperactivity Disorder (ADHD)," http://www.cdc.gov/ncbddd/adhd/data.html.

24. Ibid.

25. National Institute on Drug Abuse (NIDA), "NIDA InfoFacts: Stimulant ADHD Medications—Methylphenidate and Amphetamines," http://drugabuse.gov/infofacts/ADHD.html.

26. Haley Jones, "Adderall Addiction?," *Kansan.com*, December 4, 2008, http://www.kansan.com/news/2008/dec/04/adderall_addiction/; Abram Magomedov, "Adderall Tips: How to Convince Your Shrink You Have ADD/ADHD," *The Exiled*, June 29, 2006, http://exiledonline.com/adderall-tips-how-to-convince-your-shrink-you-have-addadhd/; Joshua Foer, "The Adderall Me: My Romance with ADHD Meds," *Slate*, May 10, 2005, http://www.slate.com/id/2118315/.

27. Raymond F. Palmer, Steven Blanchard, Zachary Stein, David Mandell, and Claudia Miller, "Environmental Mercury Release, Special Education Rates, and Autism Disorder: An Ecological Study of Texas," *Health & Place* 12, no. 2 (2006), http://www.sciencedirect.com/science?_ob=ArticleURL&_udi=B6VH5-4FH4V4B-1&_user=10&_coverDate=06%2F30%2F2006&_rdoc=1&_fmt=high&_orig=search&_origin=search&_sort=d&_docanchor=&view=c&_acct=C000050221&_version=1&_urlVersion=0&_userid=10&md5=8052d6b155f417225d02ed418708f565&searchtype=a.

28. CDC, "Attention-Deficit / Hyperactivity Disorder (ADHD)."
29. Ibid.
30. Ibid.
31. Institute of Alcohol Studies, "Does TV Encourage Teenage Drinking?," *The Food Magazine*, March 10, 2007, http://www.ias.org.uk/resources/publications/alcoholalert/alert200701/al200701_p18.html.
32. Common Sense Media, "Gossip Girl," http://www.commonsensemedia.org/tv-reviews/gossip-girl.
33. Common Sense Media, "Glee," http://www.commonsensemedia.org/tv-reviews/glee.
34. Discussion forum on Television Without Pity web site, http://forums.televisionwithoutpity.com/index.php?s=42d994bbbfac574b0858d9818171f47b&showtopic=3136417&st=495&p=8329315&#entry8329315.
35. National Association for Children of Alcoholics, "Children of Addicted Parents: Important Facts," HopeNetworks, http://www.hopenetworks.org/addiction/Children%20of%20Addicts.htm.
36. Ibid.
37. Jeanie Lerche Davis, "Researchers Identify Alcoholism Gene," WebMD, http://www.webmd.com/mental-health/news/20040526/researchers-identify-alcoholism-gene.
38. CREB, or cyclic AMP responsive element binding protein, which is known to regulate brain function during development and learning, http://www.medicalnewstoday.com/articles/8739.php

CONCLUSION   The Tyranny of Now

1. Quick Fix, http://www.quickfixurine.com/.

Bibliography

Briggs, Cynthia A., Jennifer L. Pepperell. *Women, Girls and Addiction: Celebrating the Feminine in Counseling Treatment and Recovery.* Taylor & Francis Group LLC, 2009.

Cozolino, Louis J. *The Neuroscience of Psychotherapy: Building & Rebuilding the Human Brain.* W. W. Norton Company, 2002.

Crome, Ilana, Pat Chambers, Martin Frisher, Roger Bloor, Diane Roberts. *The Relationship Between Dual Diagnosis: Substance Misuse and Dealing With Mental Health Issues.* Social Care Institute for Excellence, 2009.

Evans, Katie, J. Michael Sullivan. *Dual Diagnosis: Counseling the Mentally Ill Substance Abuser.* Second Edition, The Guilford Press, 2001.

Galanter, Marc, Herbert D. Kleber. *Psychotherapy for the Treatment of Substance Abuse.* American Psychiatric Publishing, Inc., 2011.

Gazzaniga, Michael S., Richard B. Ivry, George R. Mangun. *Cognitive Neuroscience: The Biology of the Mind.* Third Edition, W. W. Norton and Company, 2008.

Hamilton, N. Gregory. *From Inner Sources: New Directions in Object Relations Psychotherapy.* Jason Aronson, Inc., 1992.

McCance-Katz, Elinore F., H. Wesley Clark. *Key Readings in Addiction Psychiatry: Psychosocial Treatments.* American Psychiatric Association, 2006.

Pert, Candance B. *Molecules of Emotion: The Science Behind Mind-Body Medicine.* Simon and Schuster, 1999.

Phillips, Peter, Olive McKeown, Tom Sandford. *Dual Diagnosis: Practice in Context.* Blackwell Publishing Ltd., 2010.

Siegel, Allen M. *Heinz Kohut and the Psychology of the Self: Makers of Modern Psychotherapy.* Routledge, 1996.

Stohler, R., W. Rossler. *Dual Diagnosis: The Evolving Conceptual Framework.* S. Karger AG, 2005.

Index